DAY HIKES
Grand Teton
NATIONAL PARK

72 GREAT HIKES

Robert Stone
4th EDITION

Day Hike Books, Inc.
RED LODGE, MONTANA

Published by Day Hike Books, Inc.
P.O. Box 865
Red Lodge, Montana 59068

Distributed by The Globe Pequot Press
246 Goose Lane
P.O. Box 480
Guilford, CT 06437-0480
800-243-0495 (direct order) · 800-820-2329 (fax order)
www.globe-pequot.com

Photographs by Robert Stone
Design by Paula Doherty

Copyright © 2004 by Day Hike Books, Inc.
Fourth Edition
Printed in the United States of America
ISBN 1-57342-046-8
Library of Congress Control Number: 2003093223

Cover photo: The Tetons from Cottonwood Creek, Hike 37
Back cover photo: Taggart Lake, Hike 39

Table of Contents

THE HIKES

John D. Rockefeller Jr. Memorial Parkway and Flagg Ranch Area

Jackson Lake Area

Leigh Lake • Jenny Lake • Phelps Lake
and the Canyons of the Grand Tetons

Jackson Hole Valley • Northeast of Jackson

West of Jackson to Teton Pass

South of Jackson

About the Hikes
and Grand Teton National Park

Grand Teton National Park is one of the most beautiful and awe-inspiring parks in the Rocky Mountains. The craggy Teton peaks reach as high as 13,770 feet, forming a bony ridge through Wyoming along the Continental Divide. Fronting the Teton Range lies the twisting and curving Snake River, winding its way down the Jackson Hole Valley. The reflections of the Tetons gently ripple across the river's serene water.

The 96,000-acre Grand Teton National Park lies just south of Yellowstone National Park, their borders connected by the John D. Rockefeller Jr. Memorial Parkway. The Snake River's headwaters originate in Yellowstone, then the river runs the length of Grand Teton National Park. En route, the river forms the 25,000-acre Jackson Lake. Tributaries of the Snake cascade down the Teton Range and form a string of large morainal lakes along the front range. The river continues down the Jackson Hole Valley and past the town of Jackson. The Snake River watershed and the valley create an undisturbed natural corridor teeming with wildlife.

Grand Teton National Park was established in 1929. However, people have occupied the area for 12,000 years. Native American tribes, including the Blackfeet, Crow, Gros Ventre, and Shoshone, used this high valley for habitation and hunting during the warmer seasons. Mountain men, trappers, and settlers followed in the 1800s. Through the establishment of the park, the Teton Range received protection from development and overuse of its resources. Parts of the Jackson Hole area were added in 1950.

Jackson Hole is a 60-mile long valley running north and south along the Teton Range. This 10-mile wide valley runs through Grand Teton National Park and south past the town of Jackson. The valley is surrounded by rugged mountain ranges and forested wilderness areas.

The majestic Teton Range lies to the west of Jackson Hole. This range of jagged, snowcapped mountains boasts 30 peaks rising above 11,000 feet, including ten peaks above 12,000 feet. The three peaks of Grand Teton, Teewinot, and Mount Owen—known collectively as the Cathedral Group—are the centerpiece of the park. These peaks were first called "Les Trois Tetons" by French Canadian trappers in the early 1800s. (The literal translation is "the three tits.") The Teton peaks rise 3,000 to 7,000 feet from the valley floor to a high of 13,770 feet at the summit of Grand Teton.

Day Hikes In Grand Teton National Park includes a thorough cross-section of 72 day hikes throughout this park and around its perimeter. The hikes are located along the meandering Snake River and its tributaries, Jackson Lake's shoreline, up into the valleys and canyons of the Teton Range, and across the peaks straddling the Continental Divide. The trails have been chosen for their scenery, variety, and ability to be hiked within a day. All levels of hiking experience are accommodated, with hikes ranging from easy lakeshore paths to rugged canyon hikes that gain several thousand feet in elevation. Highlights include panoramic vistas, glacier-carved canyons, tumbling creeks and waterfalls, several large lakes, old-growth forests, meadows, hot springs, historical sites, prime wildlife habitats, North America's largest landslide, and two hikes atop the Jackson Hole Ski Resort.

A quick glance at the hikes' summaries will allow you to choose a hike that is appropriate to your ability and desire. An overall map on the next page identifies the locations of all the hikes. Each hike also includes its own map, driving and hiking directions, and an overview of distance/time/elevation. For further exploration, relevant maps are listed with each hike.

A few basic necessities will make your hike more enjoyable. Bring drinking water, snacks, hats, sunscreen, additional maps, and appropriate outerwear. Hike in supportive, comfortable shoes and wear layered clothing. Be prepared for inclement or variable weather caused by the high elevations. Avoid surprising bears by wearing a bear bell and hiking with a friend or group. (The Tetons have both black and grizzly bears.) Ranger stations, located throughout the park, have the latest information on weather, trail conditions, and bear activity.

Hiking in and around this national park will give you a deep appreciation of the area's beauty. You are sure to take home great memories of your hikes in the shadows of the Tetons and around Jackson Hole.

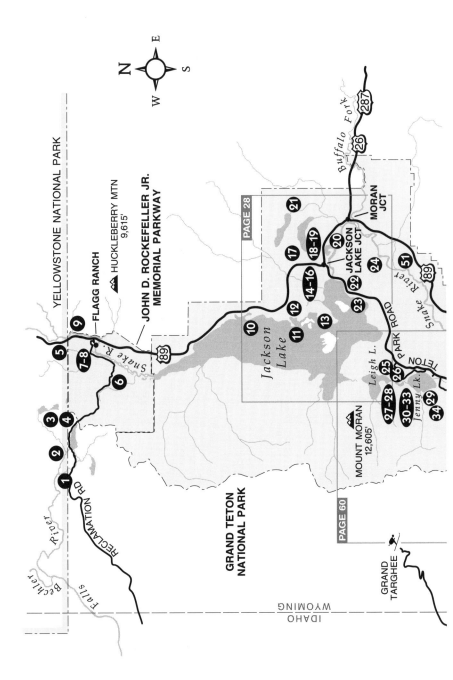

N E W S

YELLOWSTONE NATIONAL PARK

HUCKLEBERRY MTN
9,615'

FLAGG RANCH

JOHN D. ROCKEFELLER JR.
MEMORIAL PARKWAY

PAGE 28

MORAN
JCT

JACKSON
LAKE JCT

Jackson
Lake

PARK ROAD

Snake River

TETON

Leigh L.

Jenny Lk.

MOUNT MORAN
12,605'

GRAND TETON
NATIONAL PARK

PAGE 60

GRAND
TARGHEE

Snake R.

Bechler River

Falls

RECLAMATION RD

Buffalo Fork

287

26

89

89

51

IDAHO
WYOMING

1 2 3 4 5 6 7-8 9 10 11 12 13 14-16 17 18-19 20 21 22 23 24 25 26 27-28 29 30-33 34

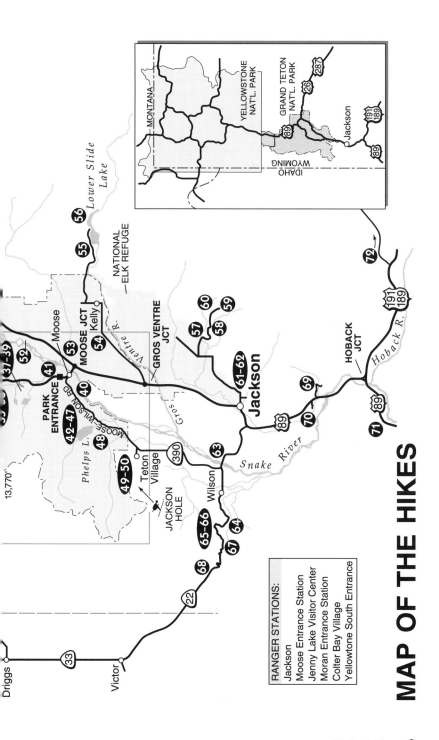

MAP OF THE HIKES

RANGER STATIONS:
Jackson
Moose Entrance Station
Jenny Lake Visitor Center
Moran Entrance Station
Colter Bay Village
Yellowtone South Entrance

Hike 1
Cascade Creek Trail to Terraced Falls

Hiking distance: 3.8 miles round trip
Hiking time: 2 hours
Elevation gain: 300 feet
Maps: U.S.G.S. Grassy Lake Reservoir
        Trails Illustrated—Old Faithful/SW Yellowstone

Summary of hike: Terraced Falls is a six-tiered cataract on the Falls River, plunging 140 feet between steep volcanic columns of rock. The trail to Terraced Falls also passes a series of magnificent waterfalls and powerful whitewater cascades along both Cascade Creek and Falls River. Cascade Creek is a short but stunning creek that connects Tillery Lake, just outside the national park in the Targhee National Forest, to Falls River. The trail parallels the creek past a steady series of whitewater cascades and waterfalls. Below the confluence of Cascade Creek and Falls River is Cascade Acres, a segmented set of rapids dropping 30 feet over a 200-yard stretch of the creek.

Driving directions: At the north end of Grand Teton National Park, turn west at the Flagg Ranch/Grassy Lake Road turnoff at Flagg Ranch Village. Make a quick right onto Grassy Lake Road (which becomes Reclamation Road en route). Continue 10.9 miles to the Grassy Lake Dam at the west end of Grassy Lake. Cross the dam and drive 1.7 miles to the trailhead on the right, just after crossing the bridge over Cascade Creek.

Hiking directions: Head downhill on the Cascade Creek Trail, a narrow, rocky road overlooking the Proposition Creek valley. Stay on the west side of Cascade Creek, entering Yellowstone National Park at 0.35 miles. Drop down to a posted junction at Cascade Creek. The right fork crosses the creek to Falls River (Hike 2). Bear left on the Terraced Falls Trail, and parallel Cascade Creek through an open lodgepole pine forest. Pass cascades over long slabs of rock, a rock grotto, and a series of waterfalls. At 1.2 miles, the trail reaches the confluence of Cascade Creek and Falls River at a wide, sweeping S-bend in the river. Follow the 80-foot wide river downstream past Cascade Acres, a 200-yard cascade by large rock formations and caves. Traverse the hillside high above the river, and slowly descend to the riverbank. The trail ends on the edge of the steep cliffs at an overlook of Terraced Falls, the river, and Birch Hills.

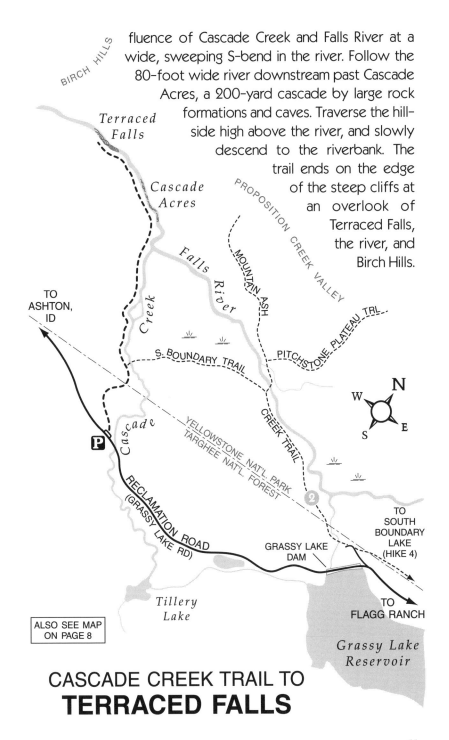

ALSO SEE MAP
ON PAGE 8

CASCADE CREEK TRAIL TO
TERRACED FALLS

Hike 2
Mountain Ash Creek—Cascade Creek Loop

Hiking distance: 4.3 mile loop
Hiking time: 2 hours
Elevation gain: 200 feet
Maps: U.S.G.S. Grassy Lake Reservoir
       Trails Illustrated—Old Faithful/SW Yellowstone

Summary of hike: The Mountain Ash Creek Trail, on the south boundary of Yellowstone National Park, begins at the spillway below the Grassy Lake Dam. The trail leads west to Mountain Ash Creek, Union Falls, Bechler Meadows, and the Falls River Basin. This hike follows the first portion of the trail to Falls River and makes a loop back along Cascade Creek.

Driving directions: At the north end of Grand Teton National Park, in the John D. Rockefeller Jr. Memorial Parkway, turn west at the Flagg Ranch/Grassy Lake Road turnoff at Flagg Ranch Village. Make a quick right onto Grassy Lake Road (which becomes Reclamation Road en route). Continue 10.9 miles to the Grassy Lake Dam at the west end of Grassy Lake. Before crossing the dam, turn right. Drive 0.2 miles downhill and park at the posted Mountain Ash Creek Trail.

Hiking directions: Cross over the spillway to the Mountain Ash Creek Trail sign. Go to the right, heading through the open forest 0.1 mile to the Yellowstone National Park boundary. Continue into the park, reaching Falls River at a half mile. Curve left and follow the river downstream to a posted junction at 1.1 mile. The Mountain Ash Creek Trail fords Falls River and continues 6.5 miles to Union Falls. Take the South Boundary Trail to the left, skirting the southwest edge of a wetland meadow. Wind through the forest and drop down to Cascade Creek at a rock wall. Cross the creek to a junction at 2 miles. The right fork parallels Cascade Creek and Falls River to Terraced Falls (Hike 1). This hike stays to the left and ascends the hill. Steadily gain elevation, leaving Yellowstone National Park, to Grassy Lake Road in the Targhee National Forest. Bear left on the unpaved road, crossing over Cascade Creek. Follow the road 1.6 miles to the Grassy Lake Dam. Cross the dam and bear left on the road, descending back to the trailhead.

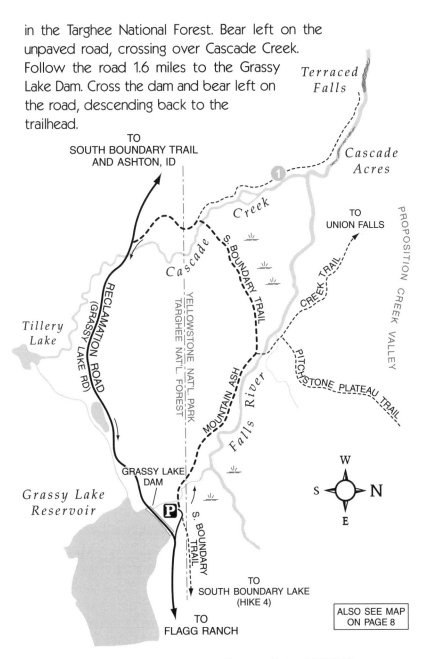

TO
SOUTH BOUNDARY TRAIL
AND ASHTON, ID

Terraced Falls

Cascade Acres

TO
UNION FALLS

PROPOSITION CREEK VALLEY

Tillery Lake

RECLAMATION ROAD
(GRASSY LAKE RD)

YELLOWSTONE NATL PARK
TARGHEE NATL. FOREST

Cascade Creek

S. BOUNDARY TRAIL

CREEK TRAIL

PITCHSTONE PLATEAU TRAIL

MOUNTAIN ASH

Falls River

Grassy Lake Reservoir

GRASSY LAKE DAM

P

S. BOUNDARY TRAIL

W
S — N
E

TO
SOUTH BOUNDARY LAKE
(HIKE 4)

TO
FLAGG RANCH

ALSO SEE MAP
ON PAGE 8

MOUNTAIN ASH CREEK–
CASCADE CREEK LOOP

Hike 3
Buela Lake

Hiking distance: 5 miles round trip
Hiking time: 2.5 hours
Elevation gain: 400 feet
Maps: U.S.G.S. Grassy Lake Reservoir
Trails Illustrated—Old Faithful/SW Yellowstone

Summary of hike: Buela Lake is a beautiful 107-acre back-country lake that sits at 7,400 feet near the south end of Yellowstone National Park. The lake is surrounded by forested hills. Yellow pond lilies grow along its marshy south end, where a stream from Hering Lake feeds the lake. The outlet stream at the northwest end of Buela Lake forms the headwaters of Falls River. Access to the trailhead is through the John D. Rockefeller Jr. Memorial Parkway and Targhee National Forest. The well-defined trail gently winds through lodgepole pines and parallels the western shoreline past two designated campsites.

Driving directions: At the north end of Grand Teton National Park, in the John D. Rockefeller Jr. Memorial Parkway, turn west at the Flagg Ranch/Grassy Lake Road turnoff at Flagg Ranch Village. Make a quick right onto Grassy Lake Road (which becomes Reclamation Road en route). Continue 9.3 miles to the unsigned Buela Lake turnout on the right side of the road. The turnout is a quarter mile past the Targhee National Forest sign.

Hiking directions: Walk past the trailhead sign, and ascend the hill to an overlook of the entire 1.8-mile-long Grassy Lake. At a half mile, atop a plateau, is a posted 4-way junction with the South Boundary Trail, which parallels the Yellowstone National Park boundary. Continue straight ahead through a new-growth forest of lodgepole pines and aspens. Cross the gently rolling terrain, heading north inside the national park. At 2.2 miles, curve east to an overlook of Buela Lake. Descend 150 feet to the forested shoreline and a view across the lake. To the right is a swampy wetland and inlet stream from Hering

Lake, a ten-minute walk to the south. The main trail curves north and follows the western shoreline past two campsites. Wild blueberries line the lakeside path, which circles the lake.

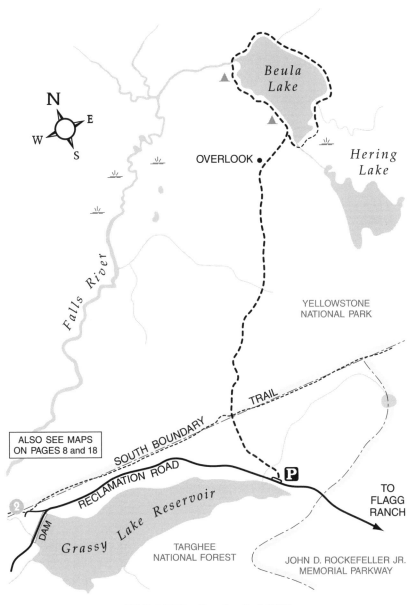

BUELA LAKE

Hike 4
South Boundary Lake
SOUTH BOUNDARY TRAIL FROM GRASSY LAKE

Hiking distance: 4.4 miles round trip
Hiking time: 2.5 hours
Elevation gain: 500 feet
Maps: U.S.G.S. Grassy Lake Reservoir and Lewis Canyon
Trails Illustrated—Old Faithful/SW Yellowstone

map
next page

Summary of hike: South Boundary Lake is an oval-shaped, 10-acre lake on the south boundary of Yellowstone National Park. The forested lake is lined with pond lilies and rimmed with lodgepole pines. Following the South Boundary Trail, the lake can be accessed from the west, near Grassy Lake, or from the east, at the south entrance to Yellowstone (Hike 5). This hike begins from Grassy Lake and climbs over a small, forested ridge to the park boundary. The trail parallels the boundary to the south edge of the lake, following the western shoreline. This hike can be combined with Hike 5 for a one-way, seven-mile shuttle hike.

Driving directions: At the north end of Grand Teton National Park, in the John D. Rockefeller Jr. Memorial Parkway, turn west at the Flagg Ranch/Grassy Lake Road turnoff at Flagg Ranch Village. Make a quick right onto Grassy Lake Road (which becomes Reclamation Road en route). Continue 9.3 miles to the unsigned Buela Lake turnout on the right side of the road. The turnout is a quarter mile past the Targhee National Forest sign.

Hiking directions: Walk past the Buela Lake Trail sign, and ascend the forested ridge to an overlook of the entire 1.8-mile-long Grassy Lake. At a half mile, atop a plateau, is a posted 4-way junction with the South Boundary Trail. The route straight ahead leads to Buela Lake (Hike 3). To the left, the South Boundary Trail leads to the Mountain Ash Creek Trail (Hike 2). Take the right fork and head east on the old access road, slowly being reclaimed by vegetation. The nearly straight path follows the south boundary of Yellowstone National Park through lodgepole pines, Engelmann spruce, and subalpine fir. At 1.5 miles, the old road becomes a single track and descends into the deep forest, reaching the southwest end of South Boundary Lake at 2 miles. The trail parallels the south side of the lake, with a few short side paths dropping down to the shoreline. This is our turnaround spot.

The trail continues 5 miles to the Snake River Ranger Station at the south entrance to Yellowstone.

Hike 5
South Boundary Lake

map next page

SOUTH BOUNDARY TRAIL FROM Y.N.P. SOUTH ENTRANCE

Hiking distance: Tanager Lake: 2 miles round trip
South Boundary Lake: 10 miles round trip
Hiking time: 1 hour to 5 hours
Elevation gain: 150 feet to 500 feet
Maps: U.S.G.S. Lewis Canyon and Grassy Lake Reservoir
Trails Illustrated—Old Faithful/SW Yellowstone

Summary of hike: The South Boundary Trail crosses the entire south end of Yellowstone National Park. This hike begins outside the south entrance gate of Yellowstone near the John D. Rockefeller Jr. Memorial Parkway and parallels the south boundary of the national park. En route to South Boundary Lake, the trail passes Tanager Lake, a 32-acre lake in a boggy, wetland meadow. The bucolic meadow is an excellent place for spotting moose and observing birds. Three miles further west is South Boundary Lake, a forested 10-acre lake lined with pond lilies. The South Boundary Trail continues west, connecting with trails to the Pitchstone Plateau, Union Falls, and the Bechler Ranger Station. This hike can be combined with Hike 4 for a one-way, seven-mile shuttle hike.

Driving directions: At the north end of Grand Teton National Park, in the John D. Rockefeller Jr. Memorial Parkway, drive 2 miles north of Flagg Ranch towards Yellowstone

National Park. Turn left across the road from the large Yellowstone National Park sign, and immediately pull into the parking spaces on the right. (The turnoff is 0.2 miles south of the Yellowstone entrance gate.)

Hiking directions: Walk up the paved service road, past the Snake River Ranger Station, to the corrals on the left. Curve around the far (north) end of the corrals to the posted trailhead. Cross the tree-dotted meadow on the faint path. Within 30 yards, the trail becomes distinct and climbs 120 feet up the hillside to the Yellowstone boundary. Follow the level tree-

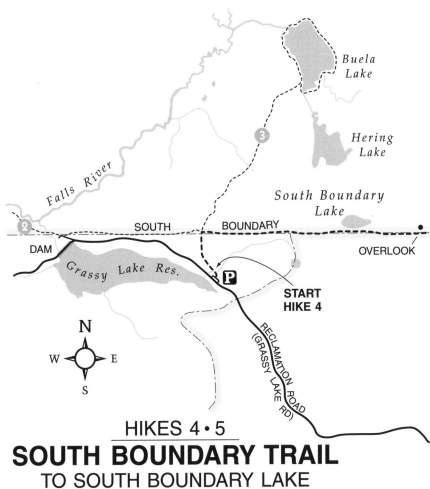

HIKES 4 • 5
SOUTH BOUNDARY TRAIL
TO SOUTH BOUNDARY LAKE

lined corridor west along the park boundary. At a half mile, make an easy, gradual descent through an open forest of young lodgepole pines. Curve south into John D. Rockefeller Jr. Memorial Parkway, and cross an old log footbridge over the Tanager Lake outlet stream. Stroll through the quiet backcountry, and cross the wetland on a long wooden footbridge. Skirt the south end of the meadow, and head back into the forest. Climb an 80-foot rise, returning to the park boundary at 1.8 miles. Continue west on the level path. At 2.5 miles the trail steadily climbs through the forest to an overlook of the Snake River valley and Huckleberry Mountain in the east. The trail parallels the south edge of South Boundary Lake at 5 miles. Short side paths drop down to the shoreline. This is our turnaround spot. The trail continues 1.5 miles to the junction with the Buela Lake Trail for a one-way, seven-mile shuttle hike with Hike 4.

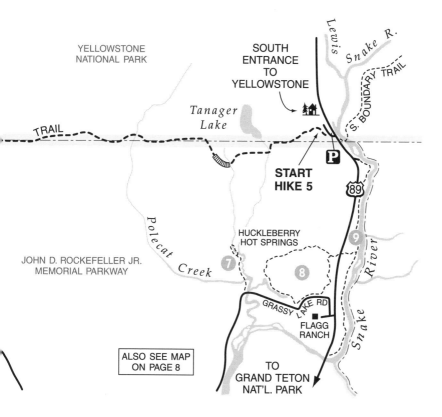

Hike 6
Glade Creek Trail
JOHN D. ROCKEFELLER JR. MEMORIAL PARKWAY

Hiking distance: 3 miles round trip
Hiking time: 1.5 hours
Elevation gain: 200 feet
Maps: U.S.G.S. Flagg Ranch
Trails Illustrated—Old Faithful/SW Yellowstone

Summary of hike: Glade Creek begins just east of Grassy Lake in the undeveloped John D. Rockefeller Jr. Memorial Parkway, a 37-square-mile corridor connecting Yellowstone National Park with Grand Teton National Park. The creek flows south, joining the Snake River above Jackson Lake. The Glade Creek Trail heads into Grand Teton National Park along the west side of Jackson Lake en route to Jenny Lake. This hike follows the first 1.5 miles to Glade Creek on an easy, well-defined path. The trail heads due south through a dense conifer forest en route to a wide valley overlooking the Snake River.

Driving directions: At the north end of Grand Teton National Park, turn west at the Flagg Ranch/Grassy Lake Road turnoff at Flagg Ranch Village. Make a quick right onto Grassy Lake Road (which becomes Reclamation Road en route). Continue 4.4 miles to the trailhead parking area on the left.

Hiking directions: Head south through the flat, open lodgepole pine forest. Cross a wooden footbridge over a small tributary stream of Glade Creek. The path heads down a long gradual descent. At 1.2 miles, views open up of the Snake River in a wide valley. Descend to the valley floor to a log footbridge over Glade Creek. This is the turnaround spot. To return, retrace your steps.

To hike further, cross the bridge and traverse the meadow along the west edge of the marshes lining the Snake River. The trail reaches the Grand Teton National Park boundary at 3.5 miles and continues along Jackson Lake. The Glade Creek Trail

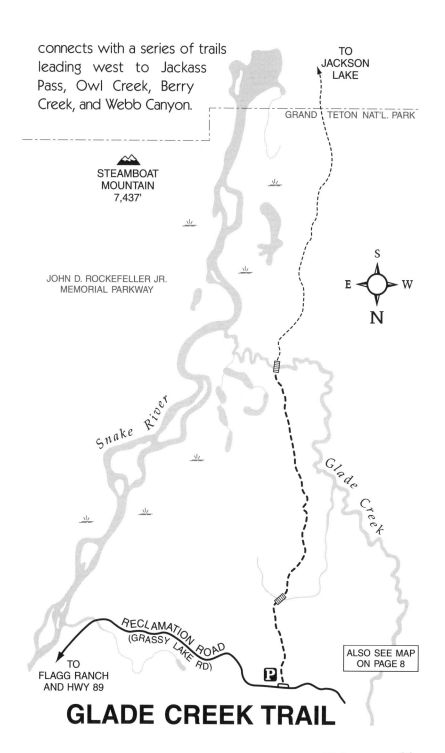

connects with a series of trails leading west to Jackass Pass, Owl Creek, Berry Creek, and Webb Canyon.

TO JACKSON LAKE

GRAND TETON NAT'L. PARK

STEAMBOAT
MOUNTAIN
7,437'

JOHN D. ROCKEFELLER JR.
MEMORIAL PARKWAY

S

E ✦ W

N

Snake River

Glade Creek

RECLAMATION ROAD
(GRASSY LAKE RD)

TO
FLAGG RANCH
AND HWY 89

P

ALSO SEE MAP
ON PAGE 8

GLADE CREEK TRAIL

Hike 7
Huckleberry Hot Springs
JOHN D. ROCKEFELLER JR. MEMORIAL PARKWAY

Hiking distance: 1 mile round trip
Hiking time: 30 minutes
Elevation gain: Level
Maps: U.S.G.S. Flagg Ranch
       Trails Illustrated—Old Faithful/SW Yellowstone

Summary of hike: Huckleberry Hot Springs is a natural hot springs in a beautiful mountain meadow between Yellowstone and Grand Teton National Parks. The springs, in excess of 100° Fahrenheit, has a series of pools, a waterfall, a grotto, and a natural bridge. The hot springs are located along a small tributary stream of Polecat Creek, which empties into the Snake River two miles downstream. This short, easy hike is a popular cross-country ski route in the winter.

Driving directions: At the north end of Grand Teton National Park, in the John D. Rockefeller Jr. Memorial Parkway, turn west at the Flagg Ranch/Grassy Lake Road turnoff at Flagg Ranch Village. Make a quick right onto Grassy Lake Road. Continue 1.1 miles to the unmarked trailhead parking pullout on the right, located immediately after crossing the bridge over Polecat Creek.

Hiking directions: From the parking pullout, hike north on the abandoned road past the "no bikes and no dogs" undesignated trail sign. After 100 yards the trail splits. Bear to the right and wade through the 20-foot wide Polecat Creek. Careful footing is advised as the current is stronger than it looks. After crossing, the trail leads into a meadow. Near the middle of the meadow is a stream. This is the beginning of the hot springs. Follow the stream to the left, heading upstream to a series of warm water pools. Return by retracing your steps.

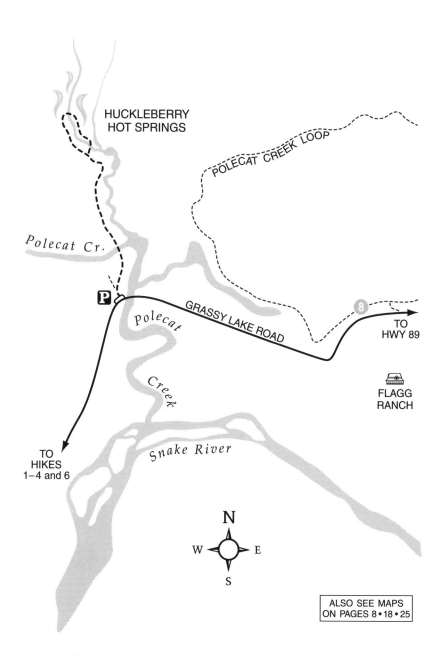

HUCKLEBERRY HOT SPRINGS

POLECAT CREEK LOOP

Polecat Cr.

P

GRASSY LAKE ROAD

Polecat

Creek

8

TO HWY 89

FLAGG RANCH

TO HIKES 1–4 and 6

Snake River

N
W — E
S

ALSO SEE MAPS ON PAGES 8 • 18 • 25

HUCKLEBERRY HOT SPRINGS
JOHN D. ROCKEFELLER JR. PARKWAY

Hike 8
Polecat Creek Loop Trail
JOHN D. ROCKEFELLER JR. MEMORIAL PARKWAY

Hiking distance: 2.3 mile loop
Hiking time: 1 hour
Elevation gain: 100 feet
Maps: U.S.G.S. Flagg Ranch
Trails Illustrated—Old Faithful/SW Yellowstone

Summary of hike: Polecat Creek begins a couple of miles northwest of Yellowstone National Park's south entrance. The creek flows south, joining the Snake River a mile west of Flagg Ranch. The Polecat Creek Loop begins at Flagg Ranch in the John D. Rockefeller Jr. Memorial Parkway. This hike is a leisurely walk with little elevation gain. The trail follows a ridge overlooking the lush marshy meadows along Polecat Creek. The wetlands are rich with waterfowl and songbirds. The trail traverses a lodgepole pine, subalpine fir, and Engelmann spruce forest.

Driving directions: At the north end of Grand Teton National Park, in the John D. Rockefeller Jr. Memorial Parkway, turn west at the Flagg Ranch/Grassy Lake Road turnoff at Flagg Ranch Village. Make a quick right onto Grassy Lake Road. Park at the northeast end of the visitor center parking lot, across from the horse stables on the south side of Grassy Lake Road.

Hiking directions: Walk 40 yards to the left (west) along Grassy Lake Road to the unsigned footpath on the right. The footpath connects with the signed Polecat Creek Loop 20 yards ahead. Bear left, parallel to Grassy Lake Road, hiking the loop clockwise through a lodgepole pine forest. Cross an unpaved service road and continue to the west. A short distance ahead, curve right and follow Polecat Creek above the wet, green meadow. At 1.3 miles, the path recrosses the service road to a signed junction with the Flagg Canyon Connector Trail on the left. Stay on the main trail to the right, completing the loop at Grassy Lake Road 0.5 miles ahead.

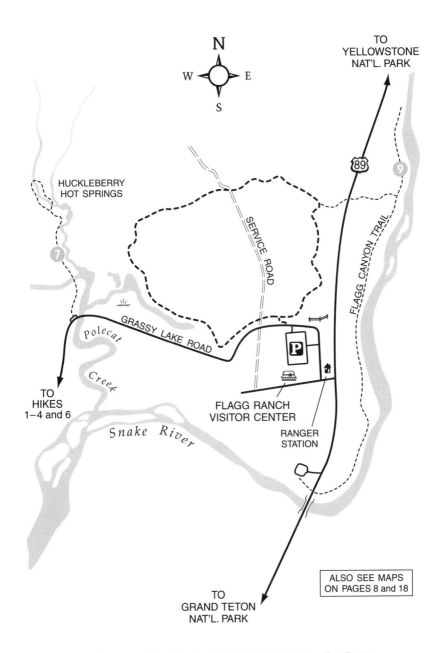

POLECAT CREEK LOOP
JOHN D. ROCKEFELLER JR. PARKWAY

Hike 9
Flagg Canyon Trail
JOHN D. ROCKEFELLER JR. MEMORIAL PARKWAY

Hiking distance: 5 miles round trip
Hiking time: 2.5 hours
Elevation gain: 100 feet
Maps: U.S.G.S. Flagg Ranch and Lewis Canyon
       Trails Illustrated—Old Faithful/SW Yellowstone

Summary of hike: The Snake River emerges from its headwaters in Yellowstone National Park, then flows through Flagg Canyon before entering Jackson Lake. This hike on the Flagg Canyon Trail follows the Snake River through the rugged, volcanic canyon along the cliff's edge.

Driving directions: From the Flagg Ranch turnoff in the John D. Rockefeller Jr. Memorial Parkway, drive south on Highway 89 (the main road) a half mile to the parking area on the right (west) side of the road. The large parking area is near the highway bridge on the north side of the Snake River.

Hiking directions: Cross the highway and pick up the trail along the north bank of the Snake River next to the Flagg Ranch Bridge. Follow the river upstream to the north. Climb a small hill, then follow the forested bluffs above the west bank of the river. At 0.8 miles, notice the cascades and waterfalls across the river, tumbling down the hillside tributary stream. The trail temporarily leaves the edge of the cliffs and winds through a conifer forest. At 1.2 miles, the path returns to the edge of the cliffs at a signed junction with the Polecat Creek Loop connector trail (Hike 8). Stay to the right, following the river past another beautiful cascade on the opposite river bank at 1.5 miles. At this point, the river narrows and swiftly flows through the steep-walled gorge of rhyolite and volcanic rock. At 2.5 miles, the trail ends at a boat launch and picnic area just south of the Yellowstone National Park boundary. Return by retracing your steps.

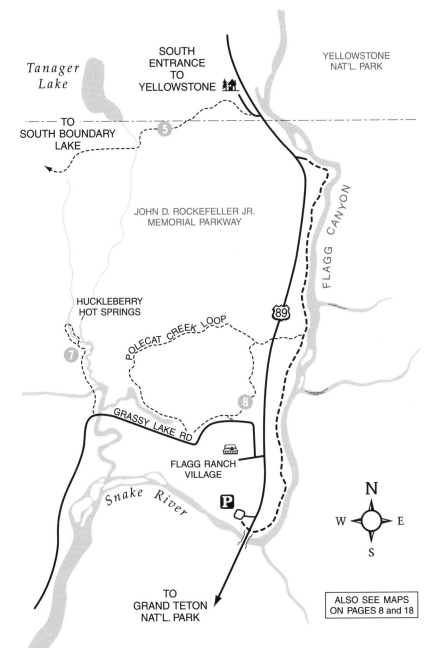

Tanager Lake

SOUTH
ENTRANCE
TO
YELLOWSTONE

YELLOWSTONE
NAT'L. PARK

TO
SOUTH BOUNDARY
LAKE

5

JOHN D. ROCKEFELLER JR.
MEMORIAL PARKWAY

FLAGG CANYON

HUCKLEBERRY
HOT SPRINGS

89

POLECAT CREEK LOOP

7

8

GRASSY LAKE RD

FLAGG RANCH
VILLAGE

Snake River

P

N
W E
S

ALSO SEE MAPS
ON PAGES 8 and 18

TO
GRAND TETON
NAT'L. PARK

FLAGG CANYON TRAIL
JOHN D. ROCKEFELLER JR. PARKWAY

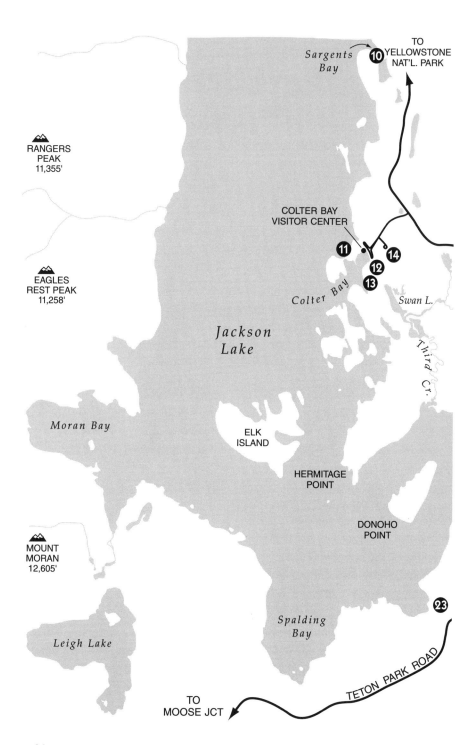

TO
YELLOWSTONE
NAT'L. PARK

Sargents
Bay

⑩

RANGERS
PEAK
11,355'

COLTER BAY
VISITOR CENTER

⑪   ⑭
   ⑫
   ⑬

EAGLES
REST PEAK
11,258'

Colter Bay

Swan L.

Jackson
Lake

Third Cr.

Moran Bay

ELK
ISLAND

HERMITAGE
POINT

DONOHO
POINT

MOUNT
MORAN
12,605'

㉓

Spalding
Bay

Leigh Lake

TO
MOOSE JCT

TETON PARK ROAD

HIKES 10–24
JACKSON LAKE AREA

Hike 10
Sargents Bay

Hiking distance: 1 to 2 miles round trip
Hiking time: 1 hour
Elevation gain: 50 feet
Maps: U.S.G.S. Colter Bay

Summary of hike: Sargents Bay is a lightly visited bay on the east shore of Jackson Lake, north of Colter Bay. The bay was formed between 1910 and 1916 when the Jackson Lake Dam raised the water level. The trail is an old wagon road that is used primarily by fishermen. It follows a gully for a quarter mile to the enclosed bay. Pebble beaches rim the shoreline, backed by the forested sloping hills.

Driving directions: From the national park entrance at Moose, continue 20 miles on Teton Park Road to Jackson Lake Junction and turn left. Drive 8.3 miles to a parking pullout on the west (left) side of the road. The unmarked trail is located 2.9 miles north of the Colter Bay turnoff and 12.7 miles south of Flagg Ranch. It is the only turnout for a long distance in either direction.

Hiking directions: Take the unsigned but distinct path down the gently sloping draw. The path meanders through an open pine forest with small meadows. Enter a dense forest along the east ridge of the ravine, then drop into and cross the ravine. Two routes lead to the shoreline at Sargents Bay. Follow the ravine to the mouth of the small cove, or climb the knoll on the path to the north edge of the cove.

To extend the hike, head north along the sandy beach to the mouth of the bay, with views across Jackson Lake. To the south, the beach leads to the southernmost end of the bay. Choose your own route and distance.

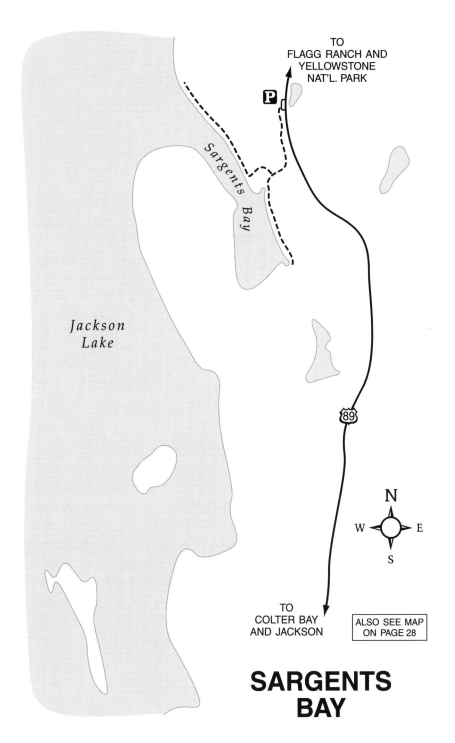

TO
FLAGG RANCH AND
YELLOWSTONE
NAT'L. PARK

P

Sargents Bay

Jackson Lake

89

N
W · E
S

TO
COLTER BAY
AND JACKSON

ALSO SEE MAP
ON PAGE 28

SARGENTS BAY

Hike 11
Lakeshore Trail at Colter Bay

Hiking distance: 2 miles round trip
Hiking time: 1 hour
Elevation gain: Level
Maps: U.S.G.S. Colter Bay
 Trails Illustrated Grand Teton National Park

Summary of hike: The Lakeshore Trail follows a section of shoreline along Colter Bay and Jackson Lake. It is an exceptional hike for water lovers. The trail crosses an isthmus and circles a forested peninsula protruding into Jackson Lake. Throughout the hike are exceptional views of the Teton Mountain Range rising above the 25,000-acre Jackson Lake.

Driving directions: From the national park entrance at Moose, continue 20 miles on Teton Park Road to Jackson Lake Junction and turn left. Drive 5.4 miles to Colter Bay Road and turn left. At the end of the road, one mile ahead, park by the Colter Bay Visitor Center.

Hiking directions: From the parking lot, walk behind the visitor center to the shoreline. Follow the paved trail to the right along the north shore of the marina through the lodgepole pine trees. At 0.5 miles is a sign marking the Lakeshore Foot Trail junction—go right. Shortly ahead, you will cross an isthmus that separates Jackson Lake and Colter Bay. Follow the trail to the left, which circles the perimeter of the peninsula in a clockwise direction. The beach at the far end of the peninsula is a wonderful area for a picnic. The trail continues along the shoreline back to the isthmus. After crossing, take the trail to the left, following the shoreline of Jackson Lake back to the Colter Bay Visitor Center.

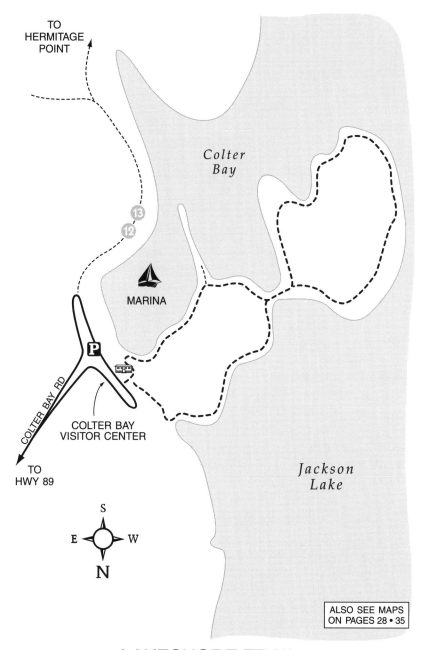

TO
HERMITAGE
POINT

*Colter
Bay*

13
12

MARINA

P

COLTER BAY RD

COLTER BAY
VISITOR CENTER

TO
HWY 89

S
E ⟡ W
N

*Jackson
Lake*

ALSO SEE MAPS
ON PAGES 28 • 35

LAKESHORE TRAIL
COLTER BAY

Hike 12
Swan Lake and Heron Pond

Hiking distance: 3 miles round trip
Hiking time: 1.5 hours
Elevation gain: Level
Maps: U.S.G.S. Colter Bay
        Trails Illustrated Grand Teton National Park

Summary of hike: The trail to Swan Lake and Heron Pond heads south from the Colter Bay Visitor Center towards Hermitage Point, a peninsula on Jackson Lake. The pristine path strolls through stands of lodgepole pines with views of Colter Bay, Jackson Lake, and the ever-present Teton peaks. Both Swan Lake and Heron Pond have abundant water lilies and water fowl, including pelicans, osprey, trumpeter swan, cranes, heron, Canada geese, and ducks. Moose and elk are frequently spotted in the area. This 3-mile loop is the beginning of the 9-mile loop to Hermitage Point (Hike 13), a full day's hike.

Driving directions: From the national park entrance at Moose, continue 20 miles on Teton Park Road to Jackson Lake Junction and turn left. Drive 5.4 miles to Colter Bay Road and turn left. At the end of the road at one mile, park by the Colter Bay Visitor Center.

Hiking directions: The trailhead is on the south end of the parking lot by the marina boat launch. Take the signed Hermitage Point Foot Trail to the right along the Colter Bay shoreline. There is a trail junction at 0.4 miles. Take the trail to the right, staying close to the shoreline. A short distance ahead is an optional loop to the Jackson Lake Overlook on the right. Both trails merge ahead at the north end of Heron Pond, one mile from the trailhead. Continue along the shore of Heron Pond to another trail junction. Follow the left trail for this hike, which loops back towards Swan Lake. (The trail to the right leads south to Hermitage Point, Hike 13.) The trail heads north, then continues along the west shore of Swan Lake. A short distance ahead,

complete the loop and return to the
Colter Bay parking lot.

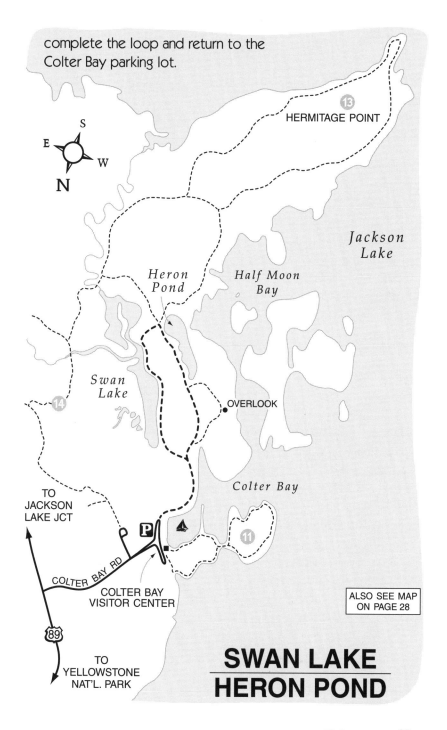

HERMITAGE POINT ⑬

Jackson Lake

Heron Pond

Half Moon Bay

OVERLOOK

Swan Lake

⑭

Colter Bay

⑪

TO
JACKSON
LAKE JCT

P

COLTER BAY RD

COLTER BAY
VISITOR CENTER

ALSO SEE MAP
ON PAGE 28

{89}

TO
YELLOWSTONE
NAT'L. PARK

SWAN LAKE
HERON POND

Hike 13
Hermitage Point Trail

Hiking distance: 8.8 mile loop
Hiking time: 4 hours
Elevation gain: 150 feet
Maps: U.S.G.S. Colter Bay, Two Ocean Lake, Jenny Lake
Trails Illustrated Grand Teton National Park

Summary of hike: The Hermitage Point Trail loops around the perimeter of a large peninsula that extends into Jackson Lake. The trail begins at Colter Bay and meanders across the rolling terrain through forests and meadows, passing ponds and creeks to the tip of the peninsula. Throughout the hike are stunning views of the Tetons and their majestic peaks. Most hikers return after the first loop (Hike 12), leaving you to explore the peninsula away from the crowds.

Driving directions: Same as Hike 12.

Hiking directions: From the south end of the parking lot, head past the boat launch to the signed Hermitage Point Foot Trail. Follow the forested path along the shoreline. At 0.4 miles, bear right towards Heron Pond. Follow the eastern shore of Heron Pond to a signed junction. The left fork leads to Swan Lake for the return route. Bear right and head south through the forest 0.8 miles towards Hermitage Point to a cut-across junction. Take the right fork down the forested peninsula, eventually giving way to the open sagebrush meadows. Cross a ridge around the narrow southern tip, and begin the return to the north past stands of Douglas fir and a primitive campsite at 4.7 miles. Follow the shoreline, then curve inland into the forest to the cut-across trail. Bear right and follow the west edge of the meadow adjacent to Third Creek. At the next junction, bear left over a small hill to the Heron Pond/Swan Lake junction. Take the right fork along the western shore of Swan Lake, returning to the first trail junction. Head right, back to the trailhead.

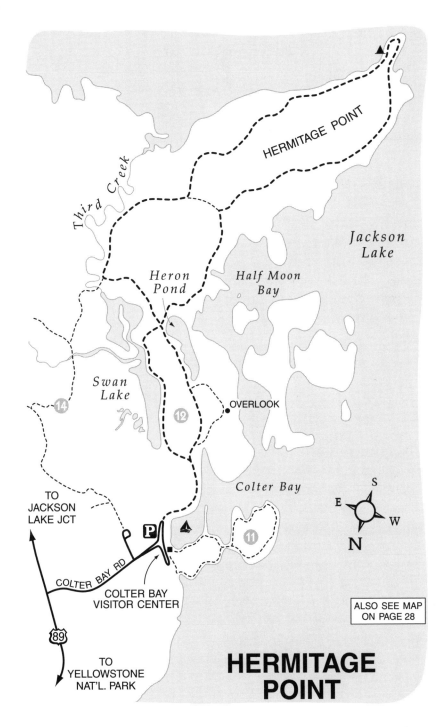

Third Creek

HERMITAGE POINT

Jackson Lake

Heron Pond

Half Moon Bay

Swan Lake

14

12

OVERLOOK

Colter Bay

TO JACKSON LAKE JCT

P

11

COLTER BAY RD

COLTER BAY VISITOR CENTER

89

TO YELLOWSTONE NAT'L. PARK

S
E — W
N

ALSO SEE MAP ON PAGE 28

HERMITAGE POINT

Hike 14
Willow Flats Loop

Hiking distance: 6.5 miles round trip
Hiking time: 3 hours
Elevation gain: Level
Maps: U.S.G.S. Colter Bay and Two Ocean Lake
  Trails Illustrated Grand Teton National Park

Summary of hike: Willow Flats is a large freshwater marsh interspersed with cottonwood, spruce, and fir forests. The extensive grassy wetlands and ponds provide a habitat for moose, elk, beaver, and waterfowl. A network of trails crosses Willow Flats, connecting Colter Bay with Jackson Lake Lodge. This hike begins and ends at the Colter Bay corrals, forming a double loop through Willow Flats. The Tetons can be seen across Jackson Lake.

Driving directions: From the national park entrance at Moose, continue 20 miles on Teton Park Road to Jackson Lake Junction and turn left. Drive 5.4 miles to Colter Bay Road and turn left. Continue 0.6 miles to a stop sign. Turn left and head 0.5 miles to the horse corrals and parking area.

Hiking directions: Follow the unpaved service road past the corrals to the signed trail for Jackson Lake Lodge. Leave the road and take the footpath to the left, beginning the first loop. Wind through the forest and cross the wide meadow in full view of the Teton Range. Traverse the side of the hill along the east edge of the meadow. Reenter the forest to a signed four-way junction at 1.2 miles, the beginning of the second loop. Bear left on the service road towards Jackson Lake Lodge. Follow the old road east through open forests, crossing Third Creek. At 2.5 miles is a signed junction. Take the right fork a short distance towards Second Creek Spring to another signed junction. Again head to the right. Cross the large grassy meadows of Willow Flats to a three-way junction. The sharp left fork leads to Swan Lake and Heron Pond. Curve to the right, crossing a long wooden bridge over Third Creek, and return to the four-way junction at the service road. Take the left fork along the old road, passing the disposal ponds, and return to the Colter Bay corrals.

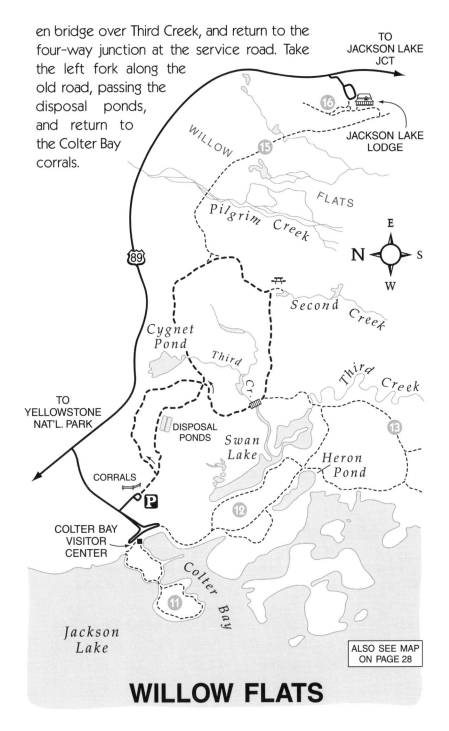

WILLOW FLATS

ALSO SEE MAP ON PAGE 28

Hike 15
Willow Flats to Second Creek

Hiking distance: 4.8 miles round trip
Hiking time: 2.5 hours
Elevation gain: Level
Maps: U.S.G.S. Two Ocean Lake
　　　　Trails Illustrated Grand Teton National Park

Summary of hike: The hike to Second Creek starts at the Jackson Lake Lodge and leads through the wildlife habitat of Willow Flats, a large marshy area with ponds and meadows. This area is frequented by moose, deer, elk, beaver, and coyotes. The trail follows a service road through stands of aspen, ponderosa pine, Douglas fir, spruce, and cottonwood trees. There are two stream crossings and spectacular views of the Teton Range.

Driving directions: From the national park entrance at Moose, continue 20 miles on Teton Park Road to Jackson Lake Junction and turn left. Drive one mile to Jackson Lodge Road and turn left. Park in the parking area near Jackson Lake Lodge.

Hiking directions: Facing towards Jackson Lake Lodge, take the service road to the left (south) of the lodge. A posted trail sign leads to an asphalt walking path. Take this path downhill to the service road, and head to the right (north) along the road. At 0.5 miles there is a log crossing over a stream. Continue 1.8 miles to a bridge that crosses the wide, rocky creek bed of Pilgrim Creek. Within minutes of crossing Pilgrim Creek, the view opens to Mount Moran. At 2.4 miles is a posted junction. Take the left fork towards Second Creek Spring. The right fork leads to Colter Bay, as does another junction 0.3 miles ahead (Hike 14). At 2.9 miles, just beyond the picnic tables, is Second Creek Spring. This is the turnaround spot. Return along the same trail.

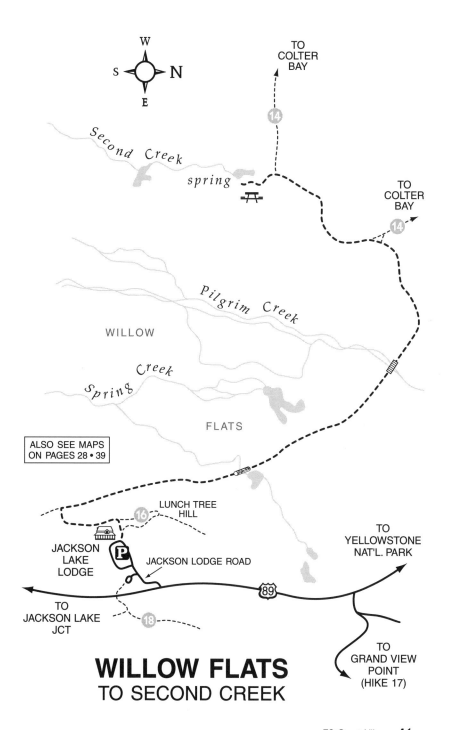

W
N
S
E

TO
COLTER
BAY

14

Second Creek

spring

TO
COLTER
BAY

14

Pilgrim Creek

WILLOW

Spring Creek

FLATS

ALSO SEE MAPS
ON PAGES 28 • 39

LUNCH TREE
HILL

16

JACKSON
LAKE
LODGE

P

JACKSON LODGE ROAD

89

TO
YELLOWSTONE
NAT'L. PARK

TO
JACKSON LAKE
JCT

18

TO
GRAND VIEW
POINT
(HIKE 17)

WILLOW FLATS
TO SECOND CREEK

Hike 16
Lunch Tree Hill Loop

Hiking distance: 0.5 mile loop to 2 miles round trip
Hiking time: 30 minutes to 1 hour
Elevation gain: 80 feet
Maps: U.S.G.S. Two Ocean Lake
   Trails Illustrated Grand Teton National Park

Summary of hike: The Lunch Tree Hill Loop is an interpretive trail that begins at Jackson Lake Lodge. The trail climbs the hill to the north and circles the sagebrush-covered blufftop. Atop the small hill is a magnificent overlook and picnic area with panoramic vistas of the Willow Flats wetlands, Jackson Lake, and the entire Teton Range, forming the backdrop. This spot is the historic site where, in 1926, John D. Rockefeller Jr. and his family had lunch with Horace Albright, then superintendent of Yellowstone Park. En route are interpretive panels about the area's history, wildlife, and plant life.

Driving directions: From the national park entrance at Moose, continue 20 miles on Teton Park Road to Jackson Lake Junction and turn left. Drive one mile to Jackson Lodge Road and turn left. Park in the parking lot near Jackson Lake Lodge.

Hiking directions: Walk through Jackson Lake Lodge and marvel at the close-up views of the entire Teton Range through the huge picture window. Head out to the walkway in front of the lodge. Follow the pathway to the right along the rail fence to the posted trailhead. Ascend the hill on the old paved path to a flat knoll at the summit. Along the path and at the summit are spectacular views of Willow Flats, Jackson Lake, the island of Donoho Point, Hermitage Point, and the awesome backdrop of the Teton Range. The trail loops around the summit. At the far end of the loop, an informal trail continues north, following the ridge along the top of the bluffs. The trail continues through sagebrush and pines to a north view of the wetland valley. Back at the self-guided loop, pass a 1953 rock memorial to John D.

Rockefeller Junior. Slowly descend, with views of prominent Signal Mountain straight ahead to the south. Stroll through an aspen grove, and return to the north side of Jackson Lake Lodge.

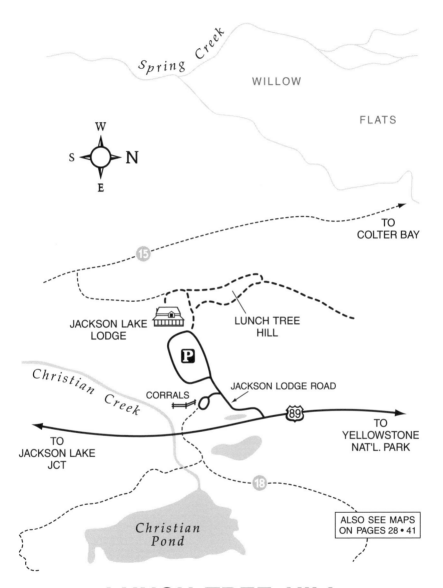

LUNCH TREE HILL

Hike 17
Grand View Point

Hiking distance: 2.2 miles round trip
Hiking time: 1 hour
Elevation gain: 600 feet
Maps: U.S.G.S. Two Ocean Lake
    Trails Illustrated Grand Teton National Park

Summary of hike: Grand View Point offers great westward views of Jackson Lake, the Teton Range, and the upper valley. To the east, Grand View Point overlooks Two Ocean Lake, Emma Matilda Lake, and the Gros Ventre Range. The forested trail is short but strenuous, gaining 600 feet in 1.1 miles, but the magnificent views at the top are well worth the effort.

Driving directions: From the national park entrance at Moose, continue 20 miles on Teton Park Road to Jackson Lake Junction and turn left. Drive 1.9 miles to an unmarked gravel road on the right. Turn right and continue 0.9 miles on the bumpy road to the trailhead parking area on the right.

Hiking directions: From the parking area, head northeast past the trailhead sign into the forest. There is a short, steep ascent for 0.2 miles to a junction. The right fork leads down to Emma Matilda Lake and Christian Pond (Hike 18). Take the left fork to Grand View Point. At 0.7 miles, the trail reaches a rocky knoll overlooking Emma Matilda Lake and Two Ocean Lake. Continue past the knoll to an unsigned trail split. The left fork leads to another knoll overlooking Jackson Lake and the Tetons. The right fork leads to Grand View Point 100 yards ahead. After enjoying the views, return by retracing your steps.

To continue from Grand View Point, the trail heads downhill for 1.3 miles to Two Ocean Lake, connecting to Hike 21.

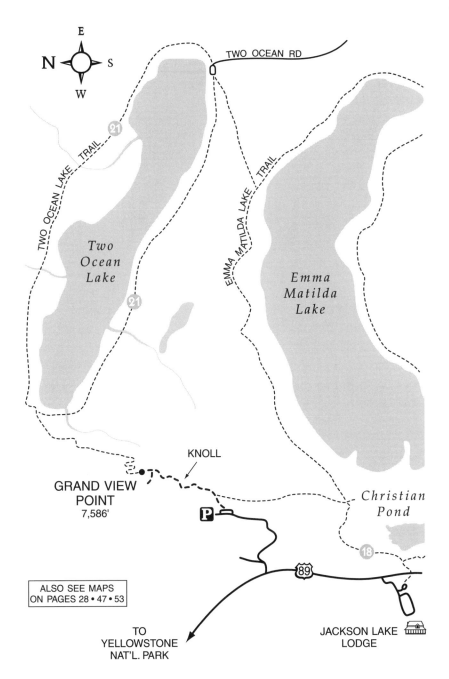

TWO OCEAN RD

N E S W

TWO OCEAN LAKE TRAIL

EMMA MATILDA LAKE TRAIL

②

Two Ocean Lake

②

Emma Matilda Lake

KNOLL

GRAND VIEW POINT
7,586'

P

Christian Pond

⑱

ALSO SEE MAPS
ON PAGES 28 • 47 • 53

89

TO
YELLOWSTONE
NAT'L. PARK

JACKSON LAKE
LODGE

GRAND VIEW POINT

Hike 18
Christian Pond Trail

Hiking distance: 3.2 miles round trip
Hiking time: 1.5 hours
Elevation gain: 250 feet
Maps: U.S.G.S. Moran and Two Ocean Lake
        Trails Illustrated Grand Teton National Park

Summary of hike: Christian Pond is a waterfowl habitat and nesting area for trumpeter swan, located across the park road from Jackson Lake Lodge. The Christian Pond Trail circles the pond through rolling hills covered in sage and stands of lodgepole pines. Open meadows offer commanding views of the Teton Range. Bring your binoculars for bird watching and wildlife observation.

Driving directions: From the national park entrance at Moose, continue 20 miles on Teton Park Road to Jackson Lake Junction and turn left. Drive one mile to Jackson Lodge Road and turn left. Drive 0.2 miles and turn left towards the corrals. Park in the first parking area on the right.

Hiking directions: From the parking lot follow the trail east, passing the horse corrals towards the highway bridge. The trail dips and crosses under the bridge to a signed trail junction in a willow-filled basin. Take the trail to the right 0.2 miles, crossing Christian Creek, to the Christian Pond Overlook. After enjoying this area, continue 0.3 miles to another signed trail junction. Take the trail to the left, which reads "via Emma Matilda Lake." Along this section of the trail are several unmarked Y-junctions. Stay left at each one. By staying left, you will loop around Christian Pond, returning to the highway bridge. Cross back under the bridge to the corrals and parking lot.

For a longer loop, combine this trail with Hike 19. Trails also lead to both Emma Matilda Lake and Two Ocean Lake. (See the map for Hike 21.)

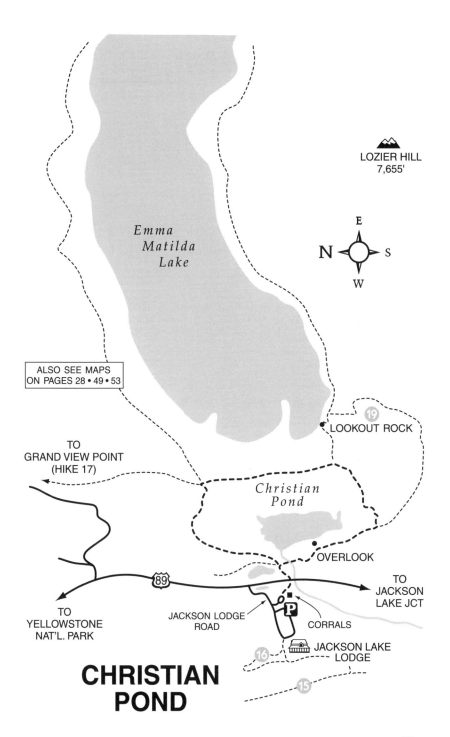

Emma
Matilda
Lake

LOZIER HILL
7,655'

E
N ✦ S
W

ALSO SEE MAPS
ON PAGES 28 • 49 • 53

TO
GRAND VIEW POINT
(HIKE 17)

⑲
● LOOKOUT ROCK

Christian
Pond

● OVERLOOK

TO
JACKSON
LAKE JCT

🛣 89

TO
YELLOWSTONE
NAT'L. PARK

JACKSON LODGE
ROAD

P

CORRALS

⑯
🏠 JACKSON LAKE
LODGE

⑮

CHRISTIAN
POND

Hike 19
Lookout Rock

Hiking distance: 3.8 miles round trip
Hiking time: 2 hours
Elevation gain: 300 feet
Maps: U.S.G.S. Moran and Two Ocean Lake
      Trails Illustrated Grand Teton National Park

Summary of hike: Lookout Rock is a gorgeous overlook on the southwest corner of Emma Matilda Lake. The hike to Lookout Rock begins near Jackson Lake Lodge and passes an overlook of Christian Pond, a waterfowl habitat and nesting area for trumpeter swan. En route are great views of Jackson Lake and the dam, the island of Donoho Point, the Teton Range, the Oxbow Bend of the Snake River, and Emma Matilda Lake.

Driving directions: Same as Hike 18.

Hiking directions: Head east past the horse corrals and under the park road to a signed junction. Bear right toward Christian Pond, weaving through the meadow marbled with waterways. Climb the knoll to the Christian Pond Overlook and continue south to a signed junction, beginning the loop. Bear right on the Oxbow Bend Overlook Trail, following the hillside ridge. As you top the hill, views open to Oxbow Bend. Continue east to a junction with the Lookout Rock Cutoff Trail on the left. Stay to the right, traversing the hillside above Oxbow Bend. At the top of the hill, the trail levels out, curves north, and enters a fir and spruce forest. Walk through meadows with stands of conifers to a signed junction at 2.3 miles on the south shore of Emma Matilda Lake. Take the left fork 0.1 mile to Lookout Rock. Climb to the overlook of the lake. After enjoying the views, descend to the west along the lakeshore to a trail split. The right fork leads 2.7 miles to Grand View Point (Hike 18). Go left, completing the loop at the next junction. Return to the right past Christian Pond and back to the trailhead.

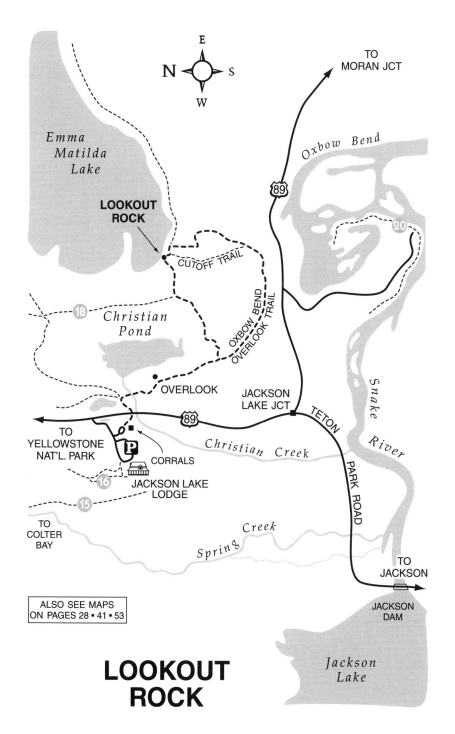

E
N — S
W

TO
MORAN JCT

Emma
Matilda
Lake

Oxbow Bend

LOOKOUT ROCK

89

CUTOFF TRAIL

20

OXBOW BEND OVERLOOK TRAIL

18

Christian
Pond

OVERLOOK

JACKSON LAKE JCT

TETON

Snake

89

River

TO
YELLOWSTONE
NAT'L. PARK

CORRALS

Christian Creek

P

JACKSON LAKE LODGE

PARK ROAD

16

15

TO
COLTER
BAY

Spring *Creek*

TO
JACKSON

ALSO SEE MAPS
ON PAGES 28 • 41 • 53

JACKSON
DAM

Jackson
Lake

LOOKOUT
ROCK

Hike 20
Oxbow Bend

Hiking distance: 1 mile round trip
Hiking time: 30 minutes
Elevation gain: Level
Maps: U.S.G.S. Moran
      Trails Illustrated Grand Teton National Park

Summary of hike: Oxbow Bend is a scenic section of the Snake River named after the U-shaped collar for an ox. The slow moving crescent-shaped bend is a superb habitat for moose, elk, beaver, muskrat, and a wide variety of waterfowl. The river curves around the northern flank of Signal Mountain near its outlet from Jackson Lake. Mount Moran of the Teton Range dominates the landscape.

Driving directions: The turnoff is located between Jackson Lake Junction and Moran Junction. From Jackson Lake Junction, drive 0.5 miles east to the unsigned road and turn right. From Moran Junction, drive 3.4 miles west to the unsigned road and turn left. Drive one mile south to the end of the unpaved road. The parking area is near the river at Cattlemans Bridge Landing.

Hiking directions: Cattlemans Bridge was built in the 1950s for herding cattle to summer pastures. From the bridge, footpaths lead downstream to the north and upstream to the west. The north route follows an open forest along the banks of a side channel of the Snake River. The path ends on a peninsula at Oxbow Bend. The west route follows the river along the base of Signal Mountain.

Across the bridge, you may stroll along the south bank of the river at the foot of Signal Mountain. Also heading south from the bridge, an unmaintained trail leaves the river and follows the east flank of Signal Mountain up to its summit (Hike 22).

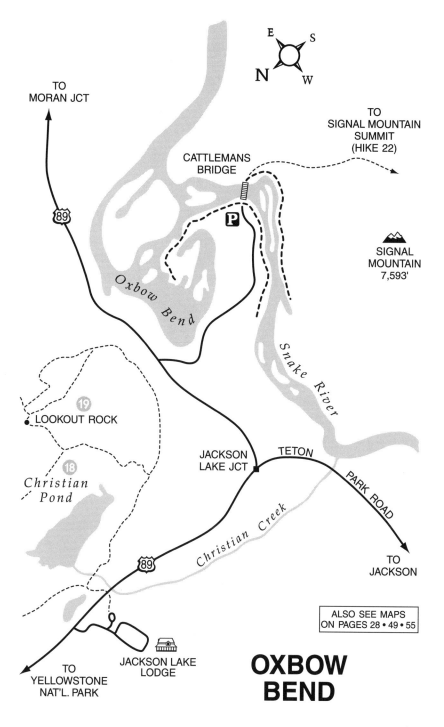

TO
MORAN JCT

E — S
N — W

TO
SIGNAL MOUNTAIN
SUMMIT
(HIKE 22)

CATTLEMANS
BRIDGE

89

P

SIGNAL
MOUNTAIN
7,593'

Oxbow Bend

Snake River

19
LOOKOUT ROCK

18

Christian Pond

JACKSON
LAKE JCT

TETON

PARK ROAD

Christian Creek

89

TO
JACKSON

ALSO SEE MAPS
ON PAGES 28 • 49 • 55

TO
YELLOWSTONE
NAT'L. PARK

JACKSON LAKE
LODGE

OXBOW
BEND

Hike 21
Two Ocean Lake

Hiking distance: 6.4 mile loop
Hiking time: 3 hours
Elevation gain: 100 feet
Maps: U.S.G.S. Two Ocean Lake
               Trails Illustrated Grand Teton National Park

Summary of hike: Two Ocean Lake is a forest-lined lake that sits in a glacier-carved depression. Snowmelt filled the depression, forming the lake as the glacier retreated. The hike around the lake traverses the rolling terrain through meadows lined with aspen groves and old-growth spruce, fir, and pines. Along the north shore are views of Jackson Lake and the Teton Range.

Driving directions: The turnoff is located between Jackson Lake Junction and Moran Junction. From Jackson Lake Junction, drive 2.7 miles east to the signed Pacific Creek Road and turn left. From Moran Junction, drive 1.3 miles west to Pacific Creek Road and turn right. Drive 2.1 miles northeast to Two Ocean Road and turn left. Continue 2.4 miles on the unpaved road to the picnic and parking area overlooking the lake at the end of the road.

Hiking directions: The signed trailhead starts to the east, where the road enters the parking area. Cross a footbridge over the lake's outlet stream, and head through the forest. Cross a meadow lined with aspens. Curve left along the northern shore of Two Ocean Lake. At several unsigned trail forks, stay to the right to avoid the lower wetlands. Follow the well-defined path west through sage-covered meadows. The trail leaves the shoreline and crosses a creek. Traverse the meadows, crossing a second creek. At the west end of the lake is a signed junction with the Grand View Point Trail. This detour to the right will add two miles to the trip and is a wonderful side trip (see Hike 17). Continue around the south side of the lake.

The path leads through the shade of a dense conifer forest, crossing two small meadows and bridges over inlet streams. The trail emerges from the forest at the parking area.

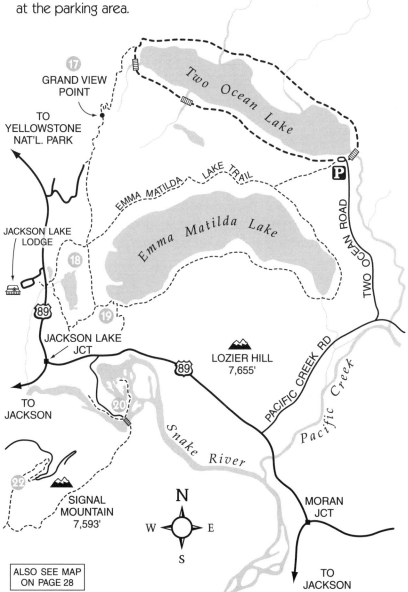

ALSO SEE MAP
ON PAGE 28

TWO OCEAN LAKE

Hike 22
Signal Mountain

Hiking distance: 5.4 miles round trip
Hiking time: 2.5 hours
Elevation gain: 700 feet
Maps: U.S.G.S. Moran
　　　　Trails Illustrated Grand Teton National Park

Summary of hike: The hike up Signal Mountain leads to Jackson Point Overlook, a scenic overlook 800 feet above the valley. To the west are views of Jackson Lake and the entire Teton Range. To the south and east is the flat glacial plain. The Snake River, Oxbow Bend, and the Teton Wilderness lay to the north. The paved Signal Mountain Road winds up to the overlook, so don't be surprised to discover people at the summit after hiking miles through the quiet solitude of the forest.

Driving directions: From the national park entrance at Moose, drive 15 miles on Teton Park Road to the signed Signal Mountain Summit Road on the right. (The road is 1.1 miles south of Signal Mountain Lodge.) Continue 1.1 miles on Signal Mountain Road to the signed trailhead on the right. Park in the parking area on the right 30 yards ahead by the pond.

Hiking directions: Head east past the trail sign along the south side of the pond covered with lily pads. Ascend a small rise through the forest to a signed junction, beginning the loop. The left fork, the Ridge Route, will be the return route. Take the right fork along the Ponds Route through the open forest of aspen and conifer. The trail weaves through the forest past two ponds on the right. At 1.7 miles, the two routes merge. Bear to the right for a one-mile ascent. Head uphill through large stands of Douglas fir. Near the top, the trail breaks out of the forest to stunning views at Jackson Point Overlook. From the overlook, a paved path leads 70 yards to a parking area. After enjoying the landscape, return one mile downhill to the signed junction with the Ridge Trail. The trail rises and drops over several ridges through the forest and meadows with excellent views of the Teton Range. At the junction with the Ponds Route, bear right, back to the trailhead.

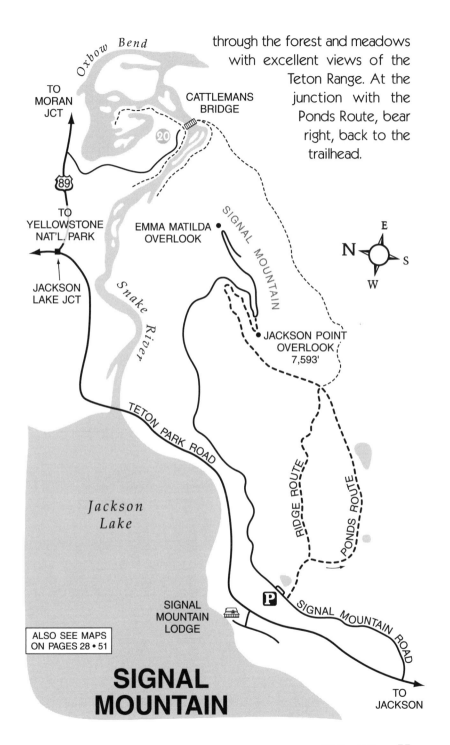

TO
MORAN
JCT

Oxbow Bend

CATTLEMANS
BRIDGE

20

89

TO
YELLOWSTONE
NAT'L. PARK

SIGNAL MOUNTAIN

EMMA MATILDA
OVERLOOK

JACKSON
LAKE JCT

Snake River

JACKSON POINT
OVERLOOK
7,593'

N   E   S   W

TETON PARK ROAD

Jackson Lake

RIDGE ROUTE

PONDS ROUTE

P

SIGNAL
MOUNTAIN
LODGE

SIGNAL MOUNTAIN ROAD

ALSO SEE MAPS
ON PAGES 28 • 51

SIGNAL
MOUNTAIN

TO
JACKSON

Hike 23
South Landing

Hiking distance: 1 mile round trip
Hiking time: 30 minutes
Elevation gain: 100 feet
Maps: U.S.G.S. Moran and Jenny Lake

Summary of hike: South Landing is a rounded cove near the south end of Jackson Lake by Signal Mountain. The secluded bay has gorgeous views of Elk Island, Donoho Point (also an island), small Marie Island, Hermitage Point, and the stunning peaks of the Teton Range. The trail descends through a lodge-pole pine forest to the shoreline, rimmed with rounded rocks.

Driving directions: From the national park entrance at Moose, continue 14.8 miles on Teton Park Road to the unsigned dirt road on the right. (The dirt road is 1.3 miles south of Signal Mountain Lodge.) The trailhead parking area is directly across from the dirt road on the west side of Teton Park Road.

Hiking directions: Follow the posted trail south across the arid, sage-covered flat. Curve right on the old road, and drop into a shaded grove of evergreens, where the road becomes a footpath. Wind downhill through the dense forest to a picnic area at the far east end of the wide, rounded cove. A full frontal view of Mount Moran sits straight west. Rounded rocks line the beach surrounding the cove, backed by a ring of trees. Follow the shoreline north as views open up of Donoho Point and Hermitage Point. Return by retracing your steps.

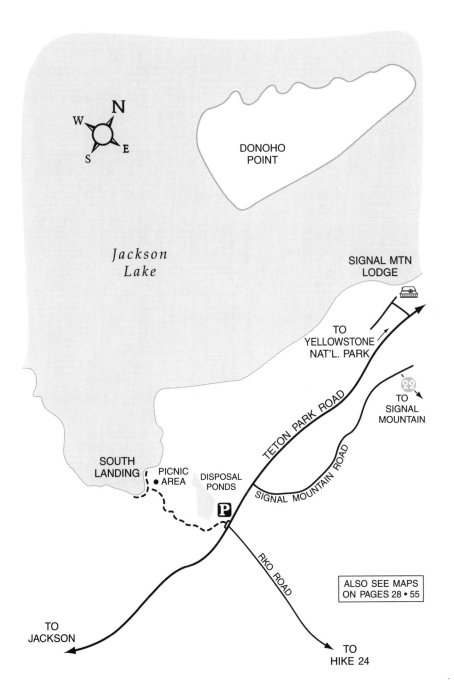

DONOHO POINT

Jackson Lake

SIGNAL MTN LODGE

TO YELLOWSTONE NAT'L. PARK

TO SIGNAL MOUNTAIN

22

TETON PARK ROAD

SIGNAL MOUNTAIN ROAD

SOUTH LANDING

PICNIC AREA

DISPOSAL PONDS

P

RKO ROAD

ALSO SEE MAPS ON PAGES 28 • 55

TO JACKSON

TO HIKE 24

SOUTH LANDING

Hike 24
Snake River Fisherman's Trail

Hiking distance: 1 to 2 miles round trip
Hiking time: 30 minutes to 1 hour
Elevation gain: Level
Maps: U.S.G.S. Moran
        Trails Illustrated Grand Teton National Park

Summary of hike: The Snake River Fisherman's Trail follows the serpentine Snake River along an unofficial angler and animal path. This hike is an opportunity to stroll along the banks of the river in the solitude of a quiet, private setting with dramatic views of the Tetons. The trail winds through stands of cottonwood, aspen, fir, pine, and spruce trees.

Driving directions: From the national park entrance at Moose, continue 14.8 miles on Teton Park Road to the unsigned dirt road on the right, the RKO Road. (The road is 1.3 miles south of Signal Mountain Lodge.) Turn right (east) and drive 3.6 miles across the open meadow to a parking area at the end of the road by the Snake River.

Hiking directions: Walk east through the tall evergreen forest on the clearly defined path to the banks of the Snake River. Unmaintained faint paths lead along the shoreline in both directions through forests and meadows. To the left, the trail heads upstream across flat sagebrush benches. To the right, the path follows the river downstream through a dense forest. (Notice the trees cut down by beavers.) At a quarter mile, the trail breaks out of the trees into an open meadow with fantastic views of the Tetons. In each direction are small islands, gravel bars, and side channels to wade across. Choose your own route and turnaround spot.

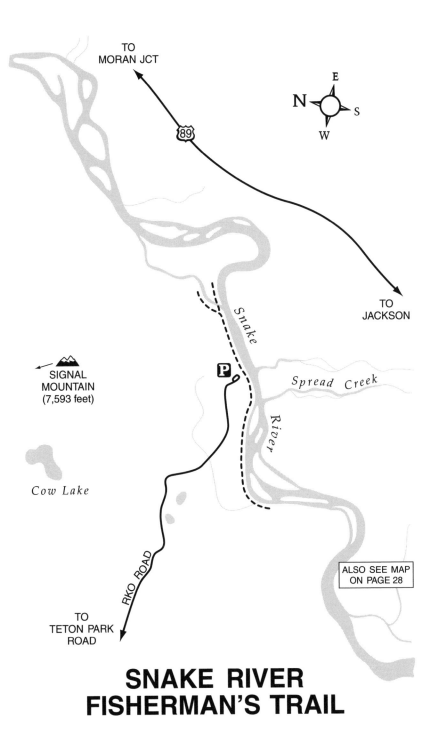

TO
MORAN JCT

89

TO
JACKSON

N
E
S
W

SIGNAL
MOUNTAIN
(7,593 feet)

Snake

Spread Creek

River

P

Cow Lake

RKO ROAD

ALSO SEE MAP
ON PAGE 28

TO
TETON PARK
ROAD

SNAKE RIVER
FISHERMAN'S TRAIL

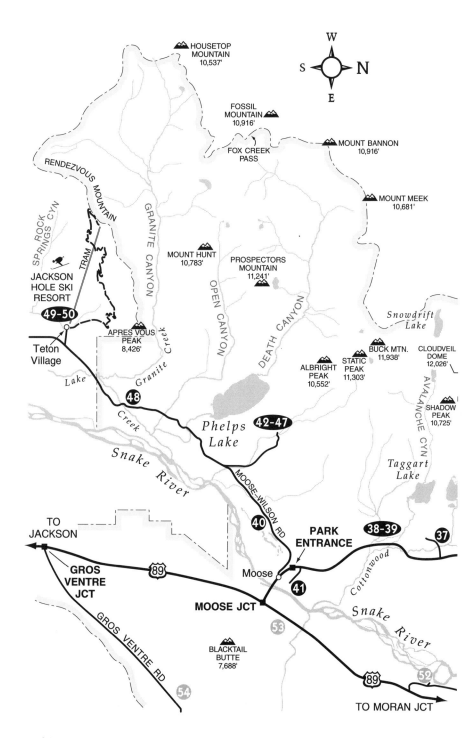

W
N
S
E

HOUSETOP
MOUNTAIN
10,537'

FOSSIL
MOUNTAIN
10,916'

MOUNT BANNON
10,916'

FOX CREEK
PASS

MOUNT MEEK
10,681'

RENDEZVOUS MOUNTAIN

ROCK SPRINGS CYN

GRANITE CANYON

MOUNT HUNT
10,783'

PROSPECTORS
MOUNTAIN
11,241'

OPEN CANYON

DEATH CANYON

Snowdrift
Lake

TRAM

JACKSON
HOLE SKI
RESORT

49-50

Teton
Village

APRES VOUS
PEAK
8,426'

Granite Creek

BUCK MTN.
11,938'

CLOUDVEIL
DOME
12,026'

ALBRIGHT
PEAK
10,552'

STATIC
PEAK
11,303'

AVALANCHE CYN

SHADOW
PEAK
10,725'

Lake

Creek

48

Phelps
Lake

42-47

Snake River

Taggart
Lake

MOOSE-WILSON RD

TO
JACKSON

40

PARK
ENTRANCE

38-39

37

Cottonwood

GROS
VENTRE
JCT

89

Moose

41

Snake River

MOOSE JCT

GROS VENTRE RD

BLACKTAIL
BUTTE
7,688'

53

89

52

54

TO MORAN JCT

60 - Day Hikes In Grand Teton National Park

LEIGH LAKE • JENNY LAKE PHELPS LAKE
CANYONS OF THE GRAND TETONS

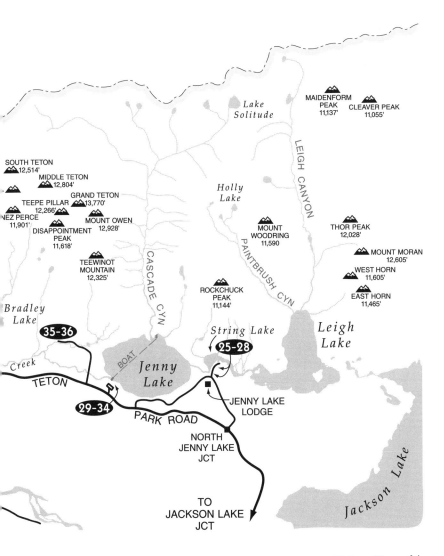

Lake Solitude

MAIDENFORM PEAK 11,137'

CLEAVER PEAK 11,055'

LEIGH CANYON

SOUTH TETON 12,514'

MIDDLE TETON 12,804'

Holly Lake

MOUNT WOODRING 11,590

THOR PEAK 12,028'

TEEPE PILLAR 12,266'

GRAND TETON 13,770'

NEZ PERCE 11,901'

MOUNT OWEN 12,928'

MOUNT MORAN 12,605'

PAINTBRUSH CYN

DISAPPOINTMENT PEAK 11,618'

WEST HORN 11,605'

TEEWINOT MOUNTAIN 12,325'

ROCKCHUCK PEAK 11,144'

EAST HORN 11,465'

CASCADE CYN

Bradley Lake

Leigh Lake

35-36

String Lake

25-28

Creek

BOAT

Jenny Lake

TETON

29-34

PARK ROAD

JENNY LAKE LODGE

NORTH JENNY LAKE JCT

TO JACKSON LAKE JCT

Jackson Lake

Hike 25
Leigh Lake to Bearpaw Lake

Hiking distance: 7.4 miles round trip
Hiking time: 3.5 hours
Elevation gain: Level
Maps: U.S.G.S. Jenny Lake
Trails Illustrated Grand Teton National Park

Summary of hike: This level hike meanders along the east shore of Leigh Lake to Bearpaw Lake, a tree-lined lake at the base of Mount Moran. The trail offers magnificent views of Mount Moran and the Cathedral Group—the three Teton peaks of Teewinot, Grand Teton, and Mount Owen. There are sandy beaches on the east side of Leigh Lake. This area is popular for canoeing, swimming, and hiking.

Driving directions: From the national park entrance at Moose, continue 10.2 miles on Teton Park Road to the North Jenny Lake Junction and turn left. Drive 0.9 miles to the String Lake picnic area and turn right. Park a short distance ahead in the parking lot.

Hiking directions: From the parking lot, several asphalt walking paths lead to the trailhead at String Lake. This trail closely follows the shore of String Lake for 0.9 miles to the southern tip of Leigh Lake. There are two trail junctions within 100 yards of each other. Take the right fork both times, staying on the Leigh Lake Trail. The trail continues north along the east shore. At 2.2 miles is the sandy East Shore Beach. As you approach the north end of Leigh Lake, a patrol cabin is on the left, then the trail splits. The right fork leads to the east side of Bearpaw Lake. The left fork curves westward around the lake to Trapper Lake. Return along the same path.

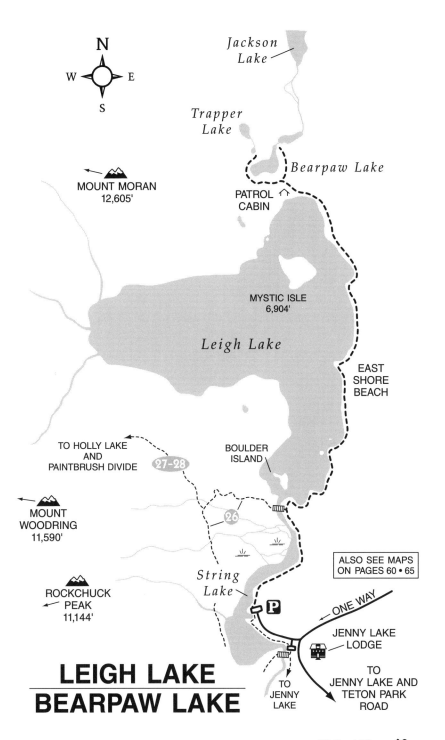

N
W E
S

Jackson Lake

Trapper Lake

Bearpaw Lake

MOUNT MORAN
12,605'

PATROL
CABIN

MYSTIC ISLE
6,904'

Leigh Lake

EAST
SHORE
BEACH

TO HOLLY LAKE
AND
PAINTBRUSH DIVIDE

27-28

BOULDER
ISLAND

MOUNT
WOODRING
11,590'

26

ALSO SEE MAPS
ON PAGES 60 • 65

String Lake

ROCKCHUCK
PEAK
11,144'

ONE WAY

P

JENNY LAKE
LODGE

TO
JENNY
LAKE

TO
JENNY LAKE AND
TETON PARK
ROAD

LEIGH LAKE
BEARPAW LAKE

Hike 26
String Lake Loop

Hiking distance: 3.6 mile loop
Hiking time: 2 hours
Elevation gain: 200 feet
Maps: U.S.G.S. Jenny Lake
Trails Illustrated Grand Teton National Park

Summary of hike: String Lake is a long and narrow lake connecting Leigh Lake to Jenny Lake along the base of the Teton peaks. String Lake is a shallow, sandy lake that warms up from the sun, making it popular for swimming. This easy hike circles String Lake, crossing bridges over streams and offering some of the best views of the Tetons.

Driving directions: From the national park entrance at Moose, continue 10.2 miles on Teton Park Road to the North Jenny Lake Junction and turn left. Drive 0.9 miles to the String Lake Picnic Area and turn right. Drive 0.1 mile and turn left into the parking lot.

Hiking directions: From the parking lot, take the trail west, crossing the wooden footbridge over the String Lake outlet stream. At 0.3 miles is a junction with the Valley Trail to Jenny Lake (Hike 29). Take the right fork on the String Lake Trail. At 0.5 miles the trail crosses a bridge over an inlet stream from Laurel Lake, sitting 700 feet above the trail. After crossing, the trail heads north. Gradually gain 200 feet to another bridge over an inlet stream. At the crest of the hill is a junction with the Paintbrush Canyon Trail (Hikes 27—28). Take the right fork, heading downhill 0.8 miles to the Leigh Lake outlet stream bridge. After crossing, take the right fork south along the shoreline of String Lake. Pass the picnic area and continue to the parking lot, completing the loop.

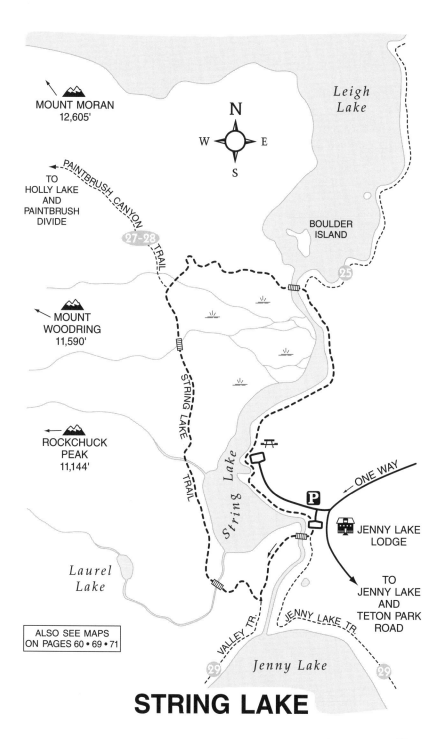

MOUNT MORAN
12,605'

Leigh Lake

N
W   E
S

PAINTBRUSH CANYON TRAIL
TO
HOLLY LAKE
AND
PAINTBRUSH
DIVIDE

27-28

BOULDER
ISLAND

25

MOUNT
WOODRING
11,590'

STRING LAKE

ROCKCHUCK
PEAK
11,144'

TRAIL

String Lake

ONE WAY

P

JENNY LAKE
LODGE

*Laurel
Lake*

TO
JENNY LAKE
AND
TETON PARK
ROAD

ALSO SEE MAPS
ON PAGES 60 • 69 • 71

VALLEY TR.

JENNY LAKE TR.

29

Jenny Lake

29

STRING LAKE

Hike 27
Paintbrush Canyon Trail to Holly Lake

Hiking distance: 12.6 miles round trip
Hiking time: 6 hours
Elevation gain: 2,500 feet
Maps: U.S.G.S. Jenny Lake and Mount Moran
        Trails Illustrated Grand Teton National Park

map
next page

Summary of hike: Holly Lake sits in a glacial cirque at the southern base of Mount Woodring in Paintbrush Canyon. Nestled in a gorgeous alpine setting, the views from the glacial tarn include Rockchuck Peak, The Jaw, Mount St. John, Leigh Lake, and Jackson Lake. The steep-walled Paintbrush Canyon, in the central part of the Teton Range, is one of the quieter, less-traveled canyons. The trail to Holly Lake begins between String and Leigh Lakes and is a steady uphill climb through the canyon.

Driving directions: Same as Hike 25.

Hiking directions: Walk north along the east shore of String Lake. Continue 0.9 miles to a bridge on the left, located just south of Leigh Lake. Cross the wooden footbridge over the connector stream between the two lakes. Head up the hillside through the woodland to a posted junction on the lower slopes of Rockchuck Peak at 1.6 miles. The left fork traverses the hillside overlooking String Lake to Jenny Lake. Bear right and head west on the Paintbrush Canyon Trail through a dense forest of lodgepole pines, Engelmann spruce, Douglas fir, and subalpine fir. The trail reaches Paintbrush Canyon Creek near the mouth of the canyon at just over 3 miles. Views extend down canyon to Leigh Lake and Mystic Isle. Enter the high-walled, glacier-carved canyon, and cross a bridge to the north bank of the creek. Continue up canyon, crossing several tributary streams from Mount Woodring. Zigzag up a series of switchbacks to a trail junction at 5.8 miles. The left fork continues through the camping zone below the divide. Take the Holly Lake Trail to the right, and climb a few switchbacks. Cross an outlet stream on the east side of a small lake, reaching the south end of Holly Lake a half mile from the junction. This is our turn-around spot.

To hike further, continue with Hike 28 to Paintbrush Divide. The divide is 1.6 miles farther and 1,300 feet higher.

Hike 28
Paintbrush Canyon Trail
to Paintbrush Divide

Hiking distance: 15.8 miles round trip
Hiking time: 8 hours
Elevation gain: 3,800 feet
Maps: U.S.G.S. Jenny Lake and Mount Moran
           Trails Illustrated Grand Teton National Park

map
next page

Summary of hike: Paintbrush Divide is in the rocky back-country of the central Teton Range. The divide lies at the upper end of Paintbrush Canyon between Leigh Canyon to the north and Cascade Canyon to the south. From the summit are sweeping vistas of the lakes beyond the mouth of the canyon, the winding Snake River, the Jackson Hole valley, and spectacular 360-degree views of the Teton peaks. Snowfields usually cover portions of the trail in the upper canyon until mid-August. The hike can be combined with Cascade Canyon (Hike 32) as a 19-mile loop.

Driving directions: Same as Hike 25.

Hiking directions: For the first 6.3 miles, follow the hiking directions to Holly Lake—Hike 27. From the lake, continue hiking southwest above the lake, and rejoin the main Paintbrush Canyon Trail in a quarter mile. Veer to the right and head uphill to the west. Watch for Grizzly Bear Lake to the north, sitting in a cirque 1,000 feet above the floor of Leigh Canyon. Traverse a rocky meadow dotted with subalpine fir and whitebark pine. Climb above timberline through meadows surrounded by high, jagged peaks and barren, craggy cliffs. Switchbacks lead through scree and snow patches to the windswept 10,700-foot divide. This is our turnaround spot.

The trail continues 2.4 miles downhill to Lake Solitude, the headwaters for the North Fork of Cascade Canyon (Hike 32). The trail then descends Cascade Canyon to Jenny Lake on the valley floor. The Cascade Canyon and Paintbrush Canyon trails can be hiked together as a 19-mile loop.

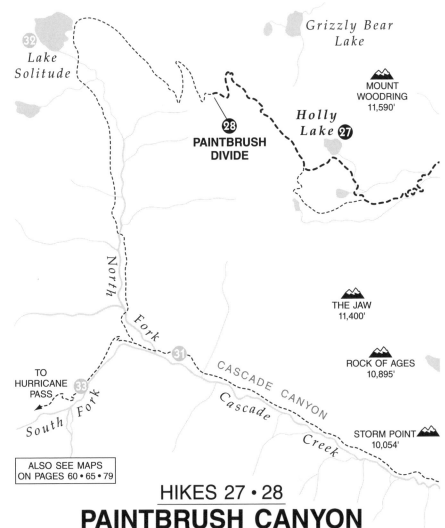

ALSO SEE MAPS
ON PAGES 60 • 65 • 79

HIKES 27 • 28
PAINTBRUSH CANYON
TO HOLLY LAKE and PAINTBRUSH DIVIDE

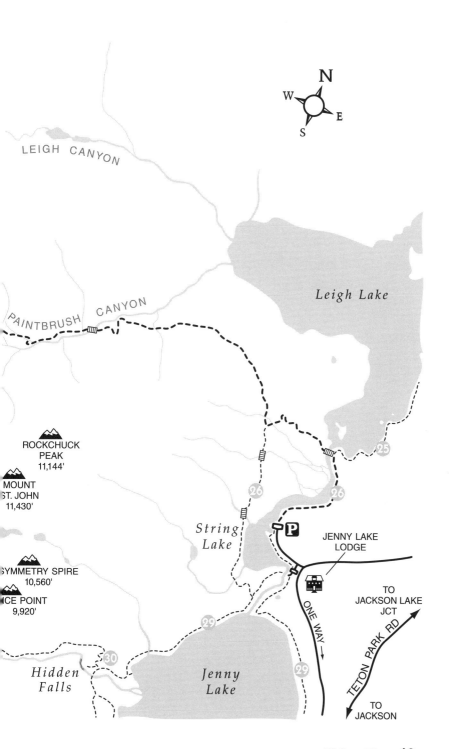

N

W E

S

LEIGH CANYON

Leigh Lake

PAINTBRUSH CANYON

ROCKCHUCK
PEAK
11,144'

MOUNT
ST. JOHN
11,430'

String
Lake

26

26

25

P

JENNY LAKE
LODGE

SYMMETRY SPIRE
10,560'

ICE POINT
9,920'

29

ONE WAY

TO
JACKSON LAKE
JCT

TETON PARK RD

Hidden
Falls

30

Jenny
Lake

29

TO
JACKSON

Hike 29
Jenny Lake Loop

Hiking distance: Via boat shuttle: 5 miles round trip
(boat shuttle leaves every 20 minutes)
Walk perimeter: 7 miles round trip
Hiking time: 2.5 hours to 4 hours
Elevation gain: Level
Maps: U.S.G.S. Jenny Lake
Trails Illustrated Grand Teton National Park

Summary of hike: Jenny Lake sits in a glacial moraine at the mouth of Cascade Canyon beneath the spectacular Teton peaks. The lake is the second largest lake in Grand Teton National Park. (Jackson Lake is the largest.) It stretches 2.5 miles along the Teton Range with a width of 1.5 miles. This popular hike circles the perimeter of gorgeous Jenny Lake in a magnificent scenic setting. The hike may be shortened two miles by taking the boat shuttle across the lake from the Jenny Lake Ranger Station to the west shore.

Driving directions: From the national park entrance at Moose, continue 7 miles on Teton Park Road to the South Jenny Lake turnoff and turn left. Park in the lot by the ranger station.

Hiking directions: From the parking lot, follow the trail to the boat dock. Take the boat shuttle to the west shore of Jenny Lake. There is a fee for the boat ride. If you prefer to hike, cross a bridge over Cottonwood Creek, and walk around the south shore of the lake. Pass the Valley Trail and Moose Ponds Trail on the left, and head to the bridge crossing Cascade Creek near the west shore dock at 2 miles. (For a side trip, take the trail to Hidden Falls and Inspiration Point—Hike 30.)

From the boat dock, the well-defined trail heads to the left towards Hidden Falls. Within minutes is a trail junction. Take the right trail, which will lead to the north end of Jenny Lake and a junction with the String Lake Trail (Hike 26). Continue on the right fork to the bridge crossing the String Lake outlet stream.

After crossing, take the trail to the right, leading around the east side of Jenny Lake back to the parking lot and ranger station.

String
Lake

JENNY LAKE
LODGE

TO
JACKSON
LAKE JCT

26

*Laurel
Lake*

ONE WAY →

JENNY LAKE TRAIL

VALLEY TRAIL

*Ribbon
Cascade*

HANGING CANYON

31-33

INSPIRATION
POINT

BOAT DOCK

*Jenny
Lake*

Cascade Cr.

BOAT SHUTTLE

30

*Hidden
Falls*

TETON PARK ROAD

HORSE TRAIL

RANGER
STATION

BOAT DOCK

P

SOUTH
JENNY LAKE
TURNOFF

*Moose
Ponds*

34

VALLEY TR.

LUPINE MEADOW RD

Cottonwood Creek

N

W ✦ E

S

ALSO SEE MAPS
ON PAGES 60 • 65 • 75

TO
JACKSON

JENNY LAKE

Hike 30
Hidden Falls and Inspiration Point
CASCADE CANYON

Hiking distance: Via boat shuttle: 1.8 miles round trip
(boat shuttle leaves every 20 minutes)
Walk south shore: 5.8 miles round trip
Hiking time: 1.5 hours
Elevation gain: 450 feet
Maps: U.S.G.S. Jenny Lake
Trails Illustrated Grand Teton National Park

Summary of hike: This hike is one of the most popular trails in the national park. Inspiration Point, on the west edge of Jenny Lake, sits atop an outcropping on a glacial bench more than 400 feet above the lake. The magnificent overlook rests near the mouth of Cascade Canyon beneath Ice Point, Storm Point, and Symmetry Spire on Mount St. John. The pinnacled Teewinot Mountain towers across the canyon. The views stretch out across Jenny Lake and the Snake River Valley to the Gros Ventre Mountains east of Jackson Hole. Hidden Falls, surrounded by spruce and fir, drops 200 feet along Cascade Creek before tumbling into Jenny Lake. This hike begins on the east shore of Jenny Lake and can be shortened two miles by taking the boat shuttle from the Jenny Lake Ranger Station to the west shore.

Driving directions: Same as Hike 29.

Hiking directions: From the parking lot, follow the trail to the boat dock. You may take the boat shuttle or hike to Hidden Falls and Inspiration Point. There is a fee for the boat shuttle, but the ride allows for great photo opportunities and shortens the hike by four miles. If you prefer to hike, walk around the south shore of Jenny Lake to Cascade Creek.

From the west shore dock, a well-defined trail to the left follows Cascade Creek to a footbridge. (Crossing the bridge will lead back two miles to the parking lot.) Take the trail to the right 0.2 miles towards Hidden Falls. Just before two other footbridges is a side trail to the left for an excellent view of the falls. Continue another half mile up switchbacks to Inspiration Point. After savoring the views, return on the same path.

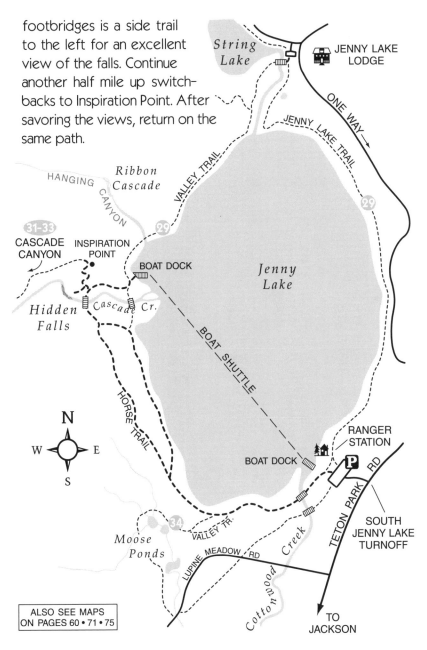

String Lake

JENNY LAKE LODGE

ONE WAY

JENNY LAKE TRAIL

29

Ribbon Cascade

HANGING CANYON

VALLEY TRAIL

31-33
CASCADE CANYON

INSPIRATION POINT

29

BOAT DOCK

Jenny Lake

Hidden Falls

Cascade Cr.

BOAT SHUTTLE

HORSE TRAIL

N
W — E
S

RANGER STATION

BOAT DOCK

P

TETON PARK RD

SOUTH JENNY LAKE TURNOFF

34

Moose Ponds

VALLEY TR.

LUPINE MEADOW RD

Cottonwood Creek

TO JACKSON

ALSO SEE MAPS ON PAGES 60 • 71 • 75

HIDDEN FALLS
INSPIRATION POINT

Hike 31
Cascade Canyon to the Canyon Fork

Hiking distance: 9.2 miles round trip
Hiking time: 5 hours
Elevation gain: 1,100 feet
Maps: U.S.G.S. Jenny Lake and Mount Moran
   Trails Illustrated Grand Teton National Park

Summary of hike: Cascade Canyon is a U-shaped, glacial-carved canyon with a wide, expansive floor and steep, mile-high walls. The hike up this canyon is one of the most popular and beautiful hikes in Grand Teton National Park. From the west end of Jenny Lake, the trail gently climbs up the magnificent canyon along Cascade Creek. The towering peaks of the Teton Range loom above throughout the hike.

Driving directions: Same as Hike 29.

Hiking directions: Follow the hiking directions to Inspiration Point—Hike 30. From Inspiration Point, take the main trail west through the forest and across talus slopes, climbing 0.6 miles to the mouth of Cascade Canyon. The trail levels out and gently heads up the wide canyon floor on the north side of Cascade Creek. Continue through open meadows, boulder fields, and forests of Engelmann spruce and Douglas fir. The steep-walled mountains tower a mile above the trail. Valhalla Canyon can be seen nestled between Mount Owen and Grand Teton, where a long, narrow cascade tumbles off the south canyon wall. At 3.6 miles from Inspiration Point, the canyon splits into a north and south fork and Cascade Creek divides. Cross a footbridge over the North Fork to a trail split a quarter mile ahead. This is our turnaround spot.

   To hike further, trails continue up both the north and south canyons. Hike 33 heads south to Hurricane Pass. Hike 32 heads north to Lake Solitude, climbing 1,200 feet in 2.7 miles, and then another 2.4 miles up to Paintbrush Divide. This hike can be combined with Hike 28 for a 19-mile loop.

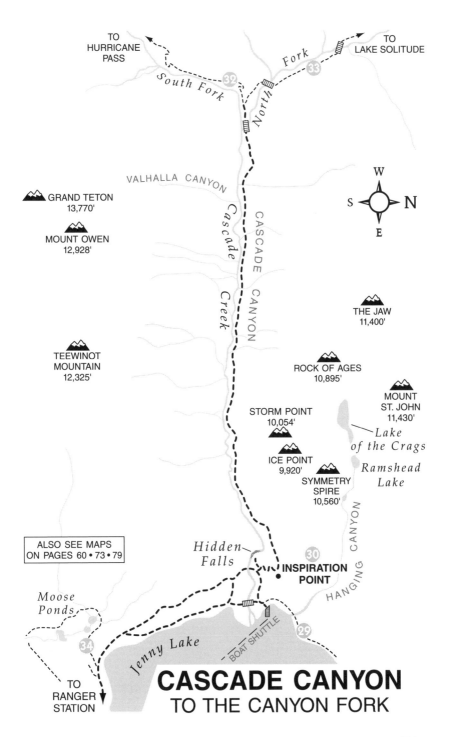

TO HURRICANE PASS

TO LAKE SOLITUDE

South Fork

North Fork

32

33

VALHALLA CANYON

△ GRAND TETON
13,770'

△ MOUNT OWEN
12,928'

Cascade Creek

Cascade

CASCADE CANYON

W
S ✦ N
E

△ THE JAW
11,400'

△ TEEWINOT MOUNTAIN
12,325'

△ ROCK OF AGES
10,895'

△ MOUNT ST. JOHN
11,430'

STORM POINT
10,054'
△

Lake of the Crags

△ ICE POINT
9,920'

△ SYMMETRY SPIRE
10,560'

Ramshead Lake

HANGING CANYON

Hidden Falls

30

INSPIRATION POINT

ALSO SEE MAPS ON PAGES 60 • 73 • 79

Moose Ponds

34

Jenny Lake

BOAT SHUTTLE

29

TO RANGER STATION

CASCADE CANYON
TO THE CANYON FORK

Hike 32
Cascade Canyon to Lake Solitude

Hiking distance: 14.5 miles round trip
Hiking time: 7 hours
Elevation gain: 2,300 feet
Maps: U.S.G.S. Jenny Lake and Mount Moran
        Trails Illustrated Grand Teton National Park

map
next page

Summary of hike: Lake Solitude is a gorgeous high mountain lake at the head of the North Fork of Cascade Canyon. The 50-acre lake sits in a glacial depression at an elevation of 9,035 feet. It is ringed by scoured mountain walls in a stunning cirque. The trail climbs up the North Fork of Cascade Canyon, in the heart of the Tetons, through sub-alpine forests, talus slopes, and meadows filled with wild flowers. Throughout the hike are magnificent views of the Cathedral Group: Teewinot Mountain, Mount Owen, and Grand Teton.

Driving directions: Same as Hike 29.

Hiking directions: Follow the hiking directions to the north fork and south fork junction of Cascade Canyon (Hike 31) at 4.6 miles. From this posted trail junction, take the right trail into the North Fork of Cascade Canyon, heading steadily uphill to the northwest. The first mile climbs through Engelmann spruce and Douglas fir, crossing two footbridges over the North Fork of Cascade Creek. Parallel the west side of the creek up the classic U-shaped, glaciated canyon, alternating between sub-alpine forest, talus slopes, and alpine meadows. The Wigwam Peaks rise high on the west wall of the canyon, and Paintbrush Divide can be seen to the right. The grade steepens as the trail zigzags up the moraine to Lake Solitude. The trail follows the east side of the lake, surrounded by the eroded, semicircular canyon walls that are sparsely dotted with some random trees. At the north shore is a world-class view down canyon of Teewinot Mountain, Mount Owen, and the Grand Teton. This is our turn-around spot.

To hike further, the trail continues via a series of steep switchbacks to Paintbrush Divide (Hike 28), gaining 1,700 feet in 2.4 miles. The trail returns to the valley floor through Paintbrush Canyon to String Lake and Jenny Lake, a 19-mile loop.

Hike 33
Cascade Canyon to Hurricane Pass

Hiking distance: 19 miles round trip
Hiking time: 10 hours
Elevation gain: 3,600 feet
Maps: U.S.G.S. Jenny Lake, Mount Moran, Grand Teton
Trails Illustrated Grand Teton National Park

map
next page

Summary of hike: Hurricane Pass sits at the head of the South Fork of Cascade Canyon. The pass is on the national park boundary, cresting at 10,372 feet. From this magnificent perch are awesome 360-degree vistas, including a back view of the Grand, Middle, and South Tetons; Table Mountain; Mount Moran; Battleship Mountain; Avalanche Divide; the limestone cliffs of The Wall; and the gradual slope of the west-facing Tetons. Below is a bird's-eye view of Schoolroom Glacier, a crescent-shaped glacier with a small lake at the toe.

Driving directions: Same as Hike 30.

Hiking directions: Follow the hiking directions to the north fork and south fork junction of Cascade Canyon (Hike 31) at 4.6 miles. The right fork climbs up the north fork to Lake Solitude (Hike 32). Take the left fork into the South Fork of Cascade Canyon. Switchbacks lead up the canyon to views of the steep east ridge of Table Mountain. Follow the tumbling whitewater of the South Fork of Cascade Creek. Pass through a few flower-filled meadows, continually gaining elevation. Two miles up the canyon, enter a forest of whitebark pine, breaking out above the treeline at 3.5 miles. Climb a quarter mile up steep switch-backs to a junction in a meadow with the Avalanche Divide Trail on the left. Stay to the right, passing through talus slopes to the

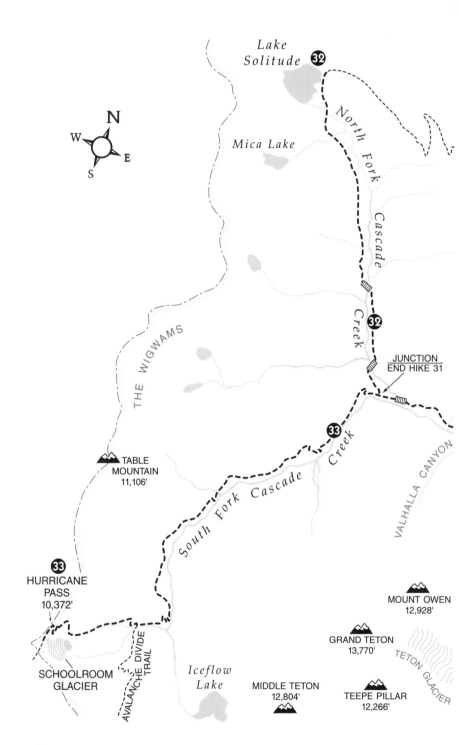

Lake
Solitude **32**

Mica Lake

North Fork

Cascade

Creek

32

JUNCTION
END HIKE 31

THE WIGWAMS

33

TABLE
MOUNTAIN
11,106'

South Fork Cascade

Creek

VALHALLA CANYON

33

HURRICANE
PASS
10,372'

MOUNT OWEN
12,928'

GRAND TETON
13,770'

TETON GLACIER

SCHOOLROOM
GLACIER

AVALANCHE DIVIDE TRAIL

*Iceflow
Lake*

MIDDLE TETON
12,804'

TEEPE PILLAR
12,266'

N
W   E
S

bottom north end of Schoolroom Glacier in a stark cirque. Zigzag up the headwall through limestone scree and possible snowfields. The trail tops out on Hurricane Pass at 9.5 miles, with sweeping views in every direction. This is our turnaround spot.

To hike further, the trail descends into Alaska Basin on the Teton Crest Trail, leaving the national park. The trail connects with Death Canyon (Hike 45) for an overnight loop hike.

28
PAINTBRUSH
DIVIDE

27
Holly Lake

PAINTBRUSH CANYON

ROCKCHUCK
PEAK
11,144'

THE JAW
11,400'

MOUNT ST. JOHN
11,430'

ALSO SEE MAPS
ON PAGES 60 • 69 • 73

Lake of the Crags

ROCK OF AGES
10,895'

Ramshead Lake

SYMMETRY SPIRE
10,560'

HANGING CANYON

ICE POINT
9,920'

STORM POINT
10,054'

INSPIRATION
POINT

CASCADE CANYON
Cascade
CANYON
Creek

29

30

*Hidden
Falls*

BOAT SHUTTLE

TEEWINOT
MOUNTAIN
12,325'

29

HIKES 32 • 33

CASCADE CANYON
TO LAKE SOLITUDE
and HURRICANE PASS

*Jenny
Lake*

Hike 34
Moose Ponds

Hiking distance: 3 miles round trip
Hiking time: 1.5 hours
Elevation gain: 150 feet
Maps: U.S.G.S. Jenny Lake and Moose
       Trails Illustrated Grand Teton National Park

Summary of hike: The Moose Ponds are a set of three ponds in a lush, stream-fed marshy bowl. The area provides an ideal habitat for moose, deer, and waterfowl. The ponds sit near the south end of Jenny Lake beneath the jagged spires of Teewinot Mountain. This loop trail begins at Jenny Lake, circles the ponds, and crosses Lupine Meadow.

Driving directions: Same as Hike 29.

Hiking directions: Take the paved path along Jenny Lake to the boat dock. Cross the footbridge over Cottonwood Creek, and take the Cascade Canyon Trail towards Hidden Falls. Follow the south edge of Jenny Lake past the boat launch to a signed junction with the Valley Trail on the left at one mile. Continue straight ahead a short distance to another signed junction near the top of the moraine. Take the Moose Ponds Loop Trail to the left to an overlook of the ponds. Descend to the willow flats and the three ponds. The path circles the ponds, crossing two footbridges and three streams. At the south end of the meadow, the trail enters a fir and spruce forest. At two miles the path breaks out of the forest into Lupine Meadows at the unpaved Lupine Meadow Road. Follow the road 30 yards to the left, and pick up the unsigned trail across the road on the right. Walk northeast through the sagebrush meadow and recross the road. The trail leads toward the Exum Climbing School. Curve left around the back of the building on a faint path. A short distance ahead is a horse bridge crossing Cottonwood Creek. Cross the creek to return to the parking lot.

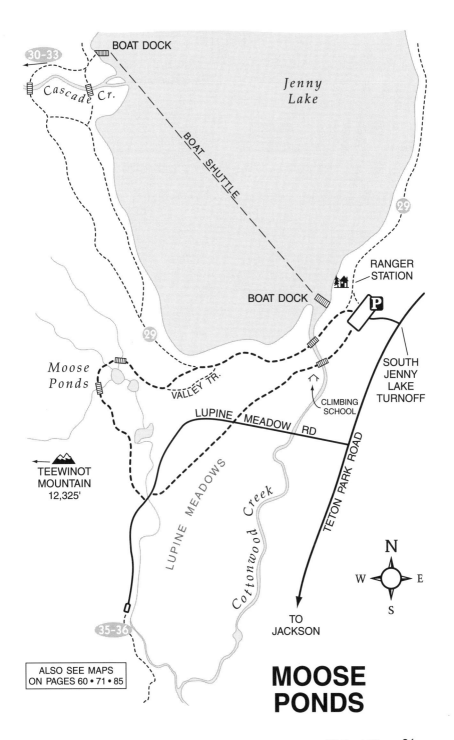

BOAT DOCK

30-33

Cascade Cr.

Jenny Lake

BOAT SHUTTLE

29

RANGER STATION

BOAT DOCK

P

SOUTH JENNY LAKE TURNOFF

29

Moose Ponds

VALLEY TR.

CLIMBING SCHOOL

LUPINE MEADOW RD

TETON PARK ROAD

TEEWINOT MOUNTAIN 12,325'

LUPINE MEADOWS

Cottonwood Creek

35-36

TO JACKSON

N
W — E
S

ALSO SEE MAPS ON PAGES 60 • 71 • 85

MOOSE PONDS

Hike 35
Surprise and Amphitheater Lakes

Hiking distance: 9.6 miles round trip
Hiking time: 5 hours
Elevation gain: 3,000 feet
Maps: U.S.G.S. Moose and Grand Teton
Trails Illustrated Grand Teton National Park

map
next page

Summary of hike: Surprise and Amphitheater Lakes sit on a bench beneath the high cliffs and snow-covered slopes of Disappointment Peak. Amphitheater Lake, at an elevation of 9,698 feet, sits in a rugged, steep-walled cirque at the eastern base of the towering peak. Surprise Lake (9,550-feet) is a circular tarn in a beautiful subalpine setting. The high mountain lakes are located only a quarter mile apart. The majestic peaks of the Teton Range, including Grand Teton, Mount Owen, and Teepe Pillar, surround the lakes. The hike begins on the valley floor in Lupine Meadows, just south of Jenny Lake, and climbs to the lakes through sage-covered meadows, forested moraines, flower-filled slopes, and alpine tundra.

Driving directions: From the national park entrance at Moose, continue 6.2 miles to Lupine Meadow Road on the left. (The road is 0.8 miles south of the South Jenny Lake turnoff.) Turn left (west) and drive 1.6 miles to the Lupine Meadows parking lot at the end of the road.

Hiking directions: Cross the sage flats, heading south to the base of the lateral moraine. Cross a bridge over the Glacier Gulch drainage, meltwater from Teton Glacier 4,000 feet above. At one mile, curve west (right) and climb the forested ridge between Glacier Gulch and Burned Wagon Gulch. At 1.7 miles, pass a signed junction with the Valley Trail on the left, which heads south to Bradley Lake. The trail begins to steeply ascend the mountain on long, sweeping switchbacks between Glacier Gulch and Garnet Canyon. Bradley and Taggart Lakes can be seen to the south and Jenny Lake to the north. Continue

climbing to a posted junction at 3 miles, located near a southern switchback and at 8,400 feet. The Garnet Canyon Trail
branches left to Spalding Falls (Hike 36). Stay to the right,
climbing more switchbacks through a forest of Douglas fir, subalpine fir, and Engelmann spruce. The trail finally levels out at 4.4
miles, where whitebark pine becomes dominant and views
open up to the surrounding mountains. In less than a quarter
mile, the trail reaches the east tip of Surprise Lake.

For a great view of Surprise Lake and the surrounding peaks,
leave the main trail, and follow the footpath south along the
lake. Climb up the 200-foot pinnacle just southeast of the lake.
Return to the main trail, and continue across the north end of
Surprise Lake for 0.2 miles to the east end of Amphitheater
Lake. The lake is nestled beneath the craggy rock walls of
Disappointment Peak, jutting up from the water's edge. The trail
follows the eastern shoreline beyond the north tip of the lake
to a saddle overlooking Glacier Gulch. Return along the same
trail.

Hike 36
Garnet Canyon to Spalding Falls

Hiking distance: 10 miles round trip
Hiking time: 5 hours
Elevation gain: 2,600 feet
Maps: U.S.G.S. Moose and Grand Teton
      Trails Illustrated Grand Teton National Park

map
next page

Summary of hike: Garnet Canyon is a narrow V-shaped
canyon in the upper Tetons. The canyon is surrounded by
Disappointment Peak, Teepe Pillar, Middle Teton, and Nez Perce.
Garnet Creek, formed by runoff from Middle Teton Glacier,
cascades through the canyon on its journey to Bradley Lake.
Spalding Falls, at an elevation of 10,000 feet, is the highest
named waterfall in the national park. The falls cascades 80 feet
off the rocky cliffs into The Meadows, a boulder-strewn
meadow framed by the jagged peaks. Below The Meadows, at
the mouth of Garnet Canyon, the creek cascades another 50

feet over Cleft Falls. The hike begins in Lupine Meadows and follows the strenuous route to Surprise and Amphitheater Lakes before veering west into Garnet Canyon. The Garnet Canyon Trail is primarily used by rock climbers tackling Middle Teton, Teepe Pillar, or Grand Teton. All off-trail hiking requires registration at the ranger station.

Driving directions: Same as Hike 35.

Hiking directions: Follow the hiking directions to Surprise and Amphitheater Lakes (Hike 35) to the posted junction with the Garnet Canyon Trail, branching off a southern switchback at 3 miles. The trail to Surprise and Amphitheater Lakes heads to the right. Take the Garnet Canyon Trail to the left and traverse the mountain. Nez Perce sits straight ahead, while Bradley and Taggart Lakes can be spotted far below. The trail soon curves right and heads into the mouth of the canyon, where views open to Middle Teton at the head of the canyon. An off-trail spur on the left drops down through a rock field to the creek below Cleft Falls. Switchbacks lead up a talus slope to the end of the designated Garnet Canyon Trail at 4.1 miles, located at a massive boulder field on the canyon floor near Cleft Falls. If you registered at the ranger station, continue on the climbers' path, traversing the boulder field while staying close to Garnet Creek. At 0.6 miles, the path reaches The Meadows, a boulder-strewn alpine meadow surrounded by the magnificent Teton peaks. At the head of the meadow, backed by the 12,804-foot Middle Teton, Spalding Falls drops off the rocky cliff to the grassy basin floor. Return along the same trail.

HIKES 35 • 36
SURPRISE and AMPHITHEATER LAKES
GARNET CANYON to SPALDING FALLS

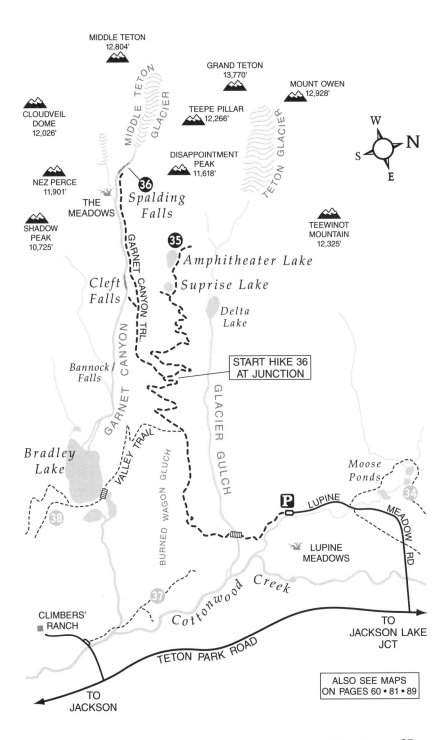

MIDDLE TETON
12,804'

GRAND TETON
13,770'

MOUNT OWEN
12,928'

MIDDLE TETON GLACIER

TEEPE PILLAR
12,266'

CLOUDVEIL
DOME
12,026'

TETON GLACIER

DISAPPOINTMENT
PEAK
11,618'

NEZ PERCE
11,901'

36

THE
MEADOWS

*Spalding
Falls*

SHADOW
PEAK
10,725'

35

TEEWINOT
MOUNTAIN
12,325'

Amphitheater Lake

GARNET CANYON TRL.

*Cleft
Falls*

Suprise Lake

*Delta
Lake*

GARNET CANYON

START HIKE 36
AT JUNCTION

*Bannock
Falls*

GLACIER GULCH

VALLEY TRAIL

*Bradley
Lake*

*Moose
Ponds*

34

BURNED WAGON GULCH

P LUPINE

MEADOW RD.

38

LUPINE
MEADOWS

37

Cottonwood Creek

CLIMBERS'
RANCH

TO
JACKSON LAKE
JCT

TETON PARK ROAD

TO
JACKSON

ALSO SEE MAPS
ON PAGES 60 • 81 • 89

W N S E

Hike 37
Cottonwood Creek

Hiking distance: 2 miles round trip
Hiking time: 1 hour
Elevation gain: Level
Maps: U.S.G.S. Moose

Summary of hike: This easy and well-defined trail parallels Cottonwood Creek into two wildflower-covered meadows along the base of the Teton Mountains (cover photo). In the first meadow is a government-owned but abandoned log structure from the old Lucas Ranch. Geraldine Lucas, who owned the ranch, died in 1938. In the second meadow is a large rock. Her ashes are buried under this rock, designated by a plaque. The views of the Tetons from both meadows are striking.

Driving directions: From the national park entrance at Moose, continue 3.7 miles on Teton Park Road to the Grand Teton Climbers' Ranch turnoff—turn left. Drive 0.3 miles to a bridge crossing Cottonwood Creek. After crossing, park in the pullout on the right.

Hiking directions: From the parking pullout, the unmarked trail heads to the north through the cottonwood trees along the west side of Cottonwood Creek. The trail crosses two small streams and a bridge over a larger inlet stream from Bradley Lake, 400 feet above. After crossing the stream, the trail enters a meadow with the historic Lucas Ranch building. Leave the trail and head east to get a closer look at the log structure. After returning, continue along the trail through the forest to a second meadow, where the trail fades out. The Geraldine Lucas rock sits in the middle of the meadow. This is our turnaround spot. Return along the same route.

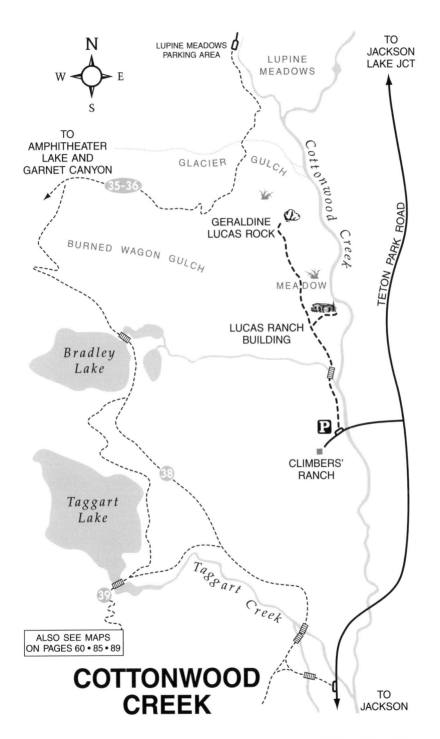

N

W   E

S

LUPINE MEADOWS
PARKING AREA

LUPINE
MEADOWS

TO
JACKSON
LAKE JCT

TO
AMPHITHEATER
LAKE AND
GARNET CANYON

GLACIER GULCH

35-36

Cottonwood Creek

GERALDINE
LUCAS ROCK

BURNED WAGON GULCH

MEADOW

TETON PARK ROAD

LUCAS RANCH
BUILDING

Bradley
Lake

38

P

Taggart
Lake

CLIMBERS'
RANCH

Taggart Creek

39

ALSO SEE MAPS
ON PAGES 60 • 85 • 89

TO
JACKSON

COTTONWOOD
CREEK

Hike 38
Bradley Lake Loop

Hiking distance: 4.8 miles round trip
Hiking time: 3 hours
Elevation gain: 520 feet
Maps: U.S.G.S. Moose and Grand Teton
       Trails Illustrated Grand Teton National Park

Summary of hike: Bradley Lake, at the base of the Tetons, was formed by a glacier flow from Garnet Canyon. The Bradley Lake Loop follows cascading Taggart Creek towards Taggart Lake. The trail climbs over a glacial moraine to Bradley Lake at the mouth of Garnet Canyon. On the return, there is an excellent overview of the area as the elevated trail perches over Taggart Lake, traversing an area burned in the 1985 Beaver Creek Fire. The new forest is thriving, as young lodgepole pines and aspens blanket the area.

Driving directions: From the national park entrance at Moose, continue 2.5 miles on Teton Park Road to the Taggart Lake Trailhead on the left. Turn left into the pullout and park.

    The trailhead is 4.5 miles south of the South Jenny Lake turnoff.

Hiking directions: From the parking lot, walk west towards the Tetons across the sagebrush flat to a signed junction at 0.2 miles. The left fork parallels Beaver Creek to Taggart Lake (Hike 39). Take the right fork and head uphill, crossing the cascading Taggart Creek via two footbridges. At 1.1 mile is another well-marked trail junction. This begins the loop portion of the hike. Go left on the Taggart Lake Trail 0.5 miles to Taggart Lake. From here the trail continues to the right along the eastern shore of the lake. Head over the moraine and through the forest towards Bradley Lake, 1.1 mile ahead. After exploring the lake along its northeast side, return to the trail junction at the south end of Bradley Lake. Take the Bradley Lake Trail to the left, and head back 2.1 miles to the parking lot.

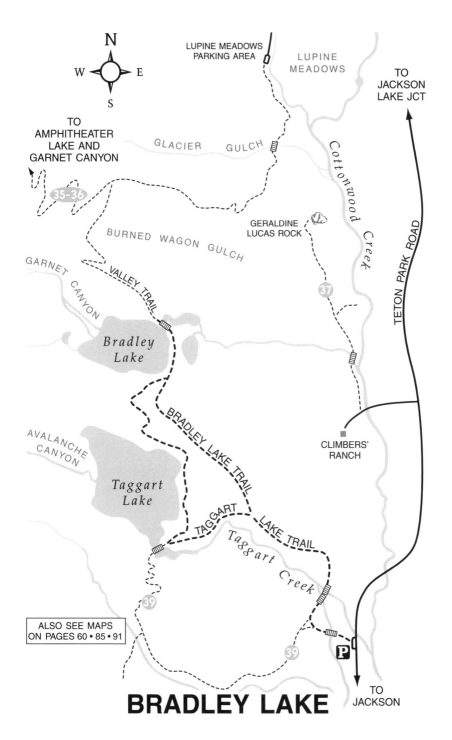

N

W • E

S

LUPINE MEADOWS
PARKING AREA

LUPINE
MEADOWS

TO
JACKSON
LAKE JCT

TO
AMPHITHEATER
LAKE AND
GARNET CANYON

GLACIER GULCH

Cottonwood Creek

35-36

GERALDINE
LUCAS ROCK

BURNED WAGON GULCH

37

GARNET CANYON

VALLEY TRAIL

TETON PARK ROAD

Bradley
Lake

BRADLEY LAKE TRAIL

CLIMBERS'
RANCH

AVALANCHE CANYON

Taggart
Lake

TAGGART LAKE TRAIL

Taggart Creek

39

ALSO SEE MAPS
ON PAGES 60 • 85 • 91

39

P

TO
JACKSON

BRADLEY LAKE

Hike 39
Taggart Lake Loop

Hiking distance: 4.4 miles round trip
Hiking time: 2 hours
Elevation gain: 300 feet
Maps: U.S.G.S. Moose and Grand Teton
　　　　Trails Illustrated Grand Teton National Park

Summary of hike: The Taggart Lake Loop is a leisurely, scenic hike at the base of the Tetons. Taggart Lake sits below the towering peaks, formed by a glacier flow from Avalanche Canyon (back cover photo). This hike circles the moraine that encloses the lake along the Beaver Creek drainage. The trail climbs over the glacial moraine to an overlook of forest-lined Taggart Lake. The hike passes through the area burned in the 1985 Beaver Creek Fire. The forest has renewed itself with young lodgepole pines and aspens.

Driving directions: Same as Hike 38.

Hiking directions: Head west across the rolling sagebrush meadow for 0.2 miles to a signed trail fork. The right fork leads to Bradley Lake (Hike 38) and is the return route for this loop hike. Take the Beaver Creek Trail to the left. In 100 yards bear left again at a second junction. The trail follows the watercourse of Beaver Creek along its north bank. Continue to a signed junction with the Valley Trail, which crosses over the creek at 1.6 miles. Head uphill to the right, with great views of the Teton Range. At the morainal ridge is an overlook of Taggart Lake. Descend to the lakeshore and cross a long wooden bridge over Taggart Creek, the outlet stream. Follow the shoreline to a signed junction. The left fork leads to Bradley Lake. Bear right, away from the lake, on the Taggart Lake Trail. Reach another junction a half mile ahead. Bear right again and follow the cascading Taggart Creek downhill. Cross two bridges over the creek, and complete the loop in the meadow. Return to the left.

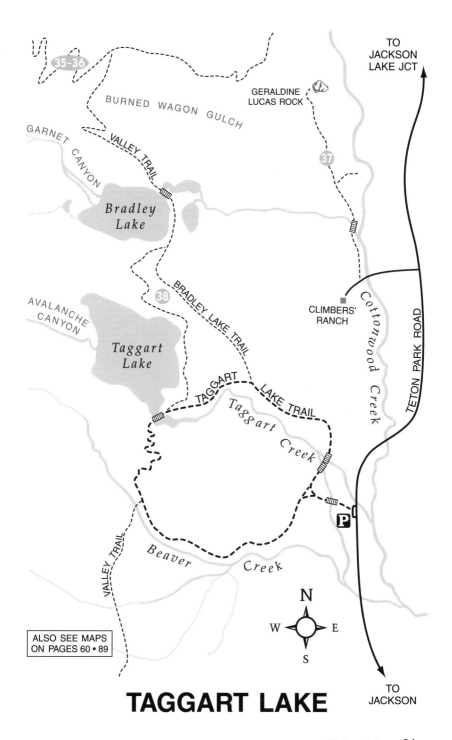

35-36

BURNED WAGON GULCH

GARNET CANYON

VALLEY TRAIL

GERALDINE
LUCAS ROCK

*Bradley
Lake*

37

BRADLEY LAKE TRAIL

38

AVALANCHE
CANYON

*Taggart
Lake*

CLIMBERS'
RANCH

Cottonwood Creek

TETON PARK ROAD

TO
JACKSON
LAKE JCT

TAGGART   LAKE TRAIL

Taggart Creek

P

VALLEY TRAIL

Beaver   Creek

N
W   E
S

ALSO SEE MAPS
ON PAGES 60 • 89

TO
JACKSON

TAGGART LAKE

Hike 40
Sawmill Ponds

Hiking distance: 1.4 miles round trip
Hiking time: 45 minutes
Elevation gain: Level
Maps: U.S.G.S. Moose

Summary of hike: The Sawmill Ponds are a series of spring-fed ponds in a wetland that provides a year-around habitat for moose and other wildlife. Beavers have dammed the stream, forming the ponds. The hike parallels the cliffs above the wetlands. From the sagebrush-covered terrace, there are bird's-eye views of the streams and ponds below, offering a great opportunity for wildlife viewing. The Teton peaks rise high above the trail to the north.

Driving directions: From the intersection of Highway 89 and Teton Park Road at Moose Junction, drive a half mile ahead to the town of Moose. On the left, across the highway from the Moose Visitor Center, is the Moose-Wilson Road to Teton Village. Turn left and continue 1.2 miles to the parking area on the left with the "Moose Habitat" information sign.

Hiking directions: Follow the wide, unsigned path at the south end of the parking area. The trail, an unpaved road that is closed to vehicles, follows the flat terrace above the Sawmill Ponds and wetlands. Side footpaths lead to overlooks and hug the edge of the cliffs parallel to the road. Continue past stands of aspens and pines. The trail ends on the sagebrush plain at an old landing strip. Return along the same route back to the trailhead.

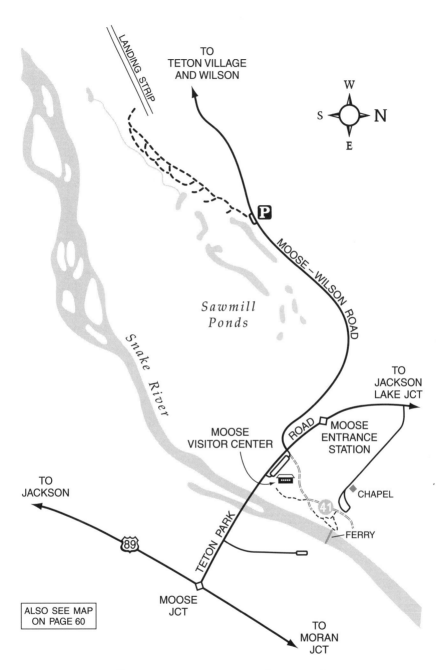

LANDING STRIP

TO
TETON VILLAGE
AND WILSON

W
S N
E

P

MOOSE – WILSON ROAD

Sawmill Ponds

Snake River

TO
JACKSON
LAKE JCT

MOOSE
VISITOR CENTER

ROAD

MOOSE
ENTRANCE
STATION

CHAPEL

41

TO
JACKSON

TETON PARK

89

FERRY

ALSO SEE MAP
ON PAGE 60

MOOSE
JCT

TO
MORAN
JCT

SAWMILL PONDS

Hike 41
Menor's Ferry—Noble Cabin

Hiking distance: 0.6 mile loop
Hiking time: 30 minutes
Elevation gain: Level
Maps: U.S.G.S. Moose
        Menor's Ferry Historic District Guide and Map

Summary of hike: Menor's Ferry and the Noble Cabin are near the park headquarters in Moose. The historical site was home to Bill Menor in the late 1800s, one of the area's first settlers. His original homestead cabin and country store, built in 1892, face the river. Adjacent to the cabin is Menor's Ferry, an in-use replica of the original ferry that was used as a vital crossing of the Snake River. The vessel consisted of a platform set on two pontoons. Pulleys were attached to the fixed cables on each shore. The river's current propelled the ferry, moving sideways across the river. The Noble Cabin was moved from Cottonwood Creek in 1918 when Maude Noble purchased Menor's Ferry. The cabin is currently a small natural history museum with an exhibit of historical photographs and a look at the life of early settlers and pioneers in Jackson Hole.

Driving directions: From the intersection of Highway 89 and Teton Park Road at Moose Junction, drive one mile on Teton Park Road to the national park entrance. Continue 0.2 miles and turn right at the first turn. Drive 0.4 miles to the parking area on the left, just past the Chapel of the Transfiguration.

    The trail can also be accessed from the Moose Visitor Center, after crossing over the Snake River but before entering the park entrance station.

Hiking directions: From the Chapel of the Transfiguration (a log chapel built in 1925), follow the paved path towards the Snake River, and begin the loop to the left. Head northeast to Menor's Cabin at the Snake River. Curve right, following the river downstream, across from Dornan's. Pass the reconstructed ferry and cable-works to a collection of covered wagons, coaches, and carriages in a log shelter. Continue downstream through a cottonwood stand to Maude Noble's cabin. Complete the loop to the right.

From the Noble Cabin, a trail continues along the Snake River to the Moose Visitor Center. A road also leads through the park employee residences to the visitor center.

MENOR'S FERRY

ALSO SEE MAPS
ON PAGES 60 • 93

Hike 42
Phelps Lake

Hiking distance: Phelps Lake Overlook: 2 miles round trip
Phelps Lake: 4 miles round trip
Hiking time: 1 to 2 hours
Elevation gain: 400 feet
Maps: U.S.G.S. Grand Teton
Trails Illustrated Grand Teton National Park

Summary of hike: This hike follows a beautifully forested trail to an overlook of the 525-acre Phelps Lake, the fourth largest lake in the park. The glacier-formed lake sits along the base of the Teton Range at the mouth of Death Canyon. Along the way to Phelps Lake are frequent springs and abundant wildflowers. From the overlook the trail descends 600 feet to the lake. Trails lead from Phelps Lake into the deep, backcountry canyons of the Tetons, including Death Canyon (Hikes 43—45), Open Canyon (Hikes 46—47), and Granite Canyon (Hike 48).

Driving directions: From the intersection of Highway 89 and Teton Park Road at Moose Junction, drive a half mile ahead to the town of Moose. On the left, across the highway from the Moose Visitor Center, is the Moose-Wilson Road to Teton Village. Turn left and continue 3 miles to the Death Canyon Trailhead turnoff on the right—turn right. Drive 1.6 miles to the end of the road, and park in the trailhead parking area.
From Teton Village, drive 5 miles north to the trailhead.

Hiking directions: Walk 0.1 mile west to a junction with the Valley Trail. The right fork heads north to the Beaver Creek Trail by Taggart Lake. Take the left fork south. Wind through a lodgepole pine, subalpine fir, and Engelmann spruce forest, crossing small streams. Leave the forest and steadily climb the moraine through a meadow to the 7,200-foot overlook at one mile. After savoring the views of Phelps Lake, the valley floor, the Gros Ventre Range, and the mouth of Death Canyon, continue down the glacial moraine via switchbacks to the junction at 1.6

miles. The Death Canyon Trail heads to the right (west), Hikes 43–45. Take the Valley Trail (left fork) to explore the west side of Phelps Lake, crossing the bridge over Death Canyon Creek. After the bridge, return along the same trail.

For a longer hike, continue up Open Canyon or Death Canyon.

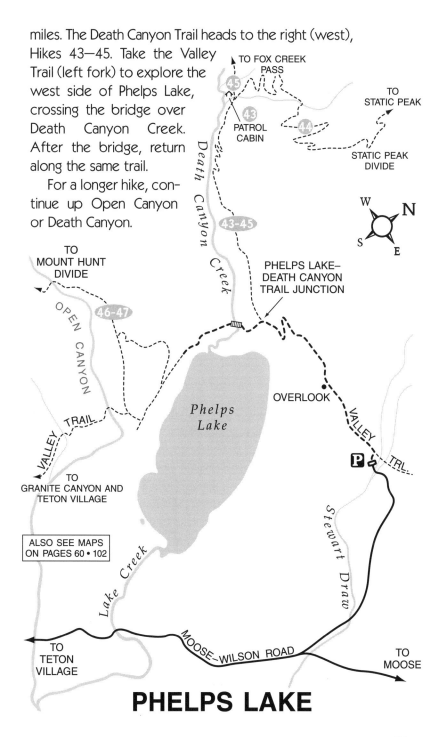

PHELPS LAKE

Hike 43
Death Canyon to Patrol Cabin

Hiking distance: 7.5 miles round trip
Hiking time: 4 hours
Elevation gain: 1,500 feet
Maps: U.S.G.S. Grand Teton
      Trails Illustrated Grand Teton National Park

map on
page 102

Summary of hike: Death Canyon is a magnificent vertical-walled canyon with some of the oldest rock in the Teton Range, dating back 2.5 billion years. The canyon is a wide, U-shaped, glacier-carved canyon with a broad floor, a gorgeous cascading creek, and jagged mountain peaks. Death Canyon Creek flows more than 2,000 feet down the canyon, from just below Fox Creek Pass, into Phelps Lake. The Death Canyon patrol cabin is a small log structure built in the 1930s. It is occupied by crews patrolling and maintaining the trails. This hike climbs through the narrow rock portals at the mouth of the canyon and traverses the north flank of the canyon to the patrol cabin.

Driving directions: From the intersection of Highway 89 and Teton Park Road at Moose Junction, drive a half mile ahead to the town of Moose. On the left, across the highway from the Moose Visitor Center, is the Moose-Wilson Road to Teton Village. Turn left and continue 3 miles to the Death Canyon Trailhead turnoff on the right—turn right. Drive 1.6 miles to the end of the road, and park in the trailhead parking area.
    From Teton Village, drive 5 miles north to the trailhead.

Hiking directions: Follow the hiking directions for Hike 42 to Phelps Lake and the Death Canyon Trail junction at 1.6 miles. From the posted junction, the Valley Trail (left fork) continues on the west side of Phelps Lake. Take the right fork and head west through the sloping, sage-covered meadow with large groves of spruce and cottonwoods. Continue towards the dramatic rock portals guarding the mouth of Death Canyon. Enter the narrow canyon, steadily gaining elevation up the north side.

Stay to the right of cascading Death Canyon Creek, and pass gorgeous rock formations beneath the towering rock walls. At 2.7 miles, climb a series of switchbacks while viewing the tumbling whitewater cascades and magnificent vistas of Phelps Lake, the Jackson Hole valley, and the Gros Ventre Range. Atop the switchbacks, the narrow, steep-walled canyon levels out and opens up into a classic U-shaped, glaciated canyon with giant slabs of granite. Follow the meandering, grass-lined stream through meadows and forest on the flat canyon floor. Keep an eye out for moose, which inhabit the area. The trail reaches the Death Canyon patrol cabin at 3.7 miles on the left, near a posted trail split. This is our turnaround spot.

To hike further, the Alaska Basin Trail branches to the right, leading to Static Peak Divide and Alaska Basin (Hike 44). The left fork continues west in Death Canyon to Fox Creek Pass, the Teton Crest Trail, and Death Canyon Shelf (Hike 45).

Hike 44
Death Canyon to the Static Peak Divide

Hiking distance: 15.4 miles round trip
Hiking time: 8 hours
Elevation gain: 4,000 feet
Maps: U.S.G.S. Grand Teton
　　　　Trails Illustrated Grand Teton National Park

map on page 102

Summary of hike: The 10,790-foot Static Peak Divide, near the national park boundary, sits between Death Canyon and Avalanche Canyon. This hike climbs up Death Canyon to the patrol cabin (Hike 43), then veers north to Static Peak Divide on the Alaska Basin Trail. Nestled beneath the sheer, jagged cliffs of the Teton Range, the strenuous Alaska Basin Trail gains 3,000 feet in four miles. From the divide are sweeping panoramic vistas of Jackson Hole, the Snake River, and the Gros Ventre Range. Beyond the divide, the trail drops into Alaska Basin in the Jedediah Smith Wilderness.

Driving directions: Same as Hike 43.

Hiking directions: Follow the hiking directions to Phelps Lake and up Death Canyon to the junction near the Death Canyon patrol cabin at 3.7 miles (Hike 43). The left fork stays in Death Canyon, leading up to Death Canyon Shelf and Fox Creek Pass (Hike 45). Take the right fork, leaving Death Canyon on the Alaska Basin Trail towards Static Peak Divide. At just over 4 miles, the path begins steep switchbacks. Climb the open, then wooded, slope through groves of subalpine fir, Engelmann spruce, and whitebark pine, staying to the west side of the drainage. Cross the stream at 5.3 miles and continue uphill. At 6.8 miles, the trail reaches a 10,200-foot saddle between Static Peak and Albright Peak. Side paths scramble up to the summit, with vistas of the canyon and the Jackson Hole valley. The main trail curves north (left) and follows the rocky ridge across loose talus for nearly a mile to Static Peak Divide at 7.7 miles. An unofficial quarter-mile side path scrambles 500 feet up the southern slope of Static Peak to the 11,303-foot summit. This is our turnaround spot.

To hike further, the trail descends past the southwest flank of Buck Mountain and beyond the park boundary into Alaska Basin.

Hike 45
Death Canyon to Fox Creek Pass

Hiking distance: 18.4 miles round trip
Hiking time: 9 hours
Elevation gain: 3,100 feet
Maps: U.S.G.S. Grand Teton and Mount Bannon
　　　　　Trails Illustrated Grand Teton National Park

map
next page

Summary of hike: Death Canyon to Fox Creek Pass is the longest hike in this book. It requires having much stamina and leaving early, or planning the hike as an overnight trek. The 9,560-foot pass is at the boundary of Grand Teton National Park and the Jedediah Smith Wilderness on the crest of the

Teton Range. The trail climbs up Death Canyon to Fox Creek Pass and the expansive Death Canyon Shelf at the head of the canyon. Death Canyon Shelf forms a towering wall on the north side of the upper canyon, surrounded by jagged 10,000-foot peaks. The shelf is an impressive limestone wall with thick horizontal stripes that stretches three miles between Fox Creek Pass and Mount Meek.

Driving directions: Same as Hike 43.

Hiking directions: Follow the hiking directions to Phelps Lake and up Death Canyon to the junction near the Death Canyon patrol cabin at 3.7 miles (Hike 43). The right fork leads up to Static Peak Divide and Alaska Basin (Hike 44). Take the left fork towards Fox Creek Pass, staying in Death Canyon. Follow the north side of the meandering, willow-lined Death Canyon Creek through the large meadow, a prime habitat for moose. A half mile beyond the cabin, pass a beautiful cascade flowing out of Rimrock Lake 2,000 feet above to the south. Cross two footbridges over the creek, entering the Death Canyon camping zone. For the next mile, climb through a forest of spruce and fir, reaching a flower-covered meadow with huge granite slabs. At 6 miles, the trail curves south to views of the upper canyon. Follow the drainage beneath the awesome Death Canyon Shelf on the north canyon wall. Cross a bridge to the south side of the creek at 6.6 miles, and traverse the open meadows. Cross a few small bridges over tributary streams, and climb out of the camping zone at the headwaters of Death Canyon Creek. Climb the open slopes with the aid of switchbacks, reaching the 9,560-foot Fox Creek Pass on the Teton Crest at the boundary between Grand Teton National Park and the Jedediah Smith Wilderness. Atop the crest is a posted junction with the Teton Crest Trail, the turnaround point for this hike. Return along the same trail.

The 38-mile Teton Crest Trail continues south to Ski Lake (Hike 66) and north to Cascade Canyon (Hike 33) along the spine of the Teton Range.

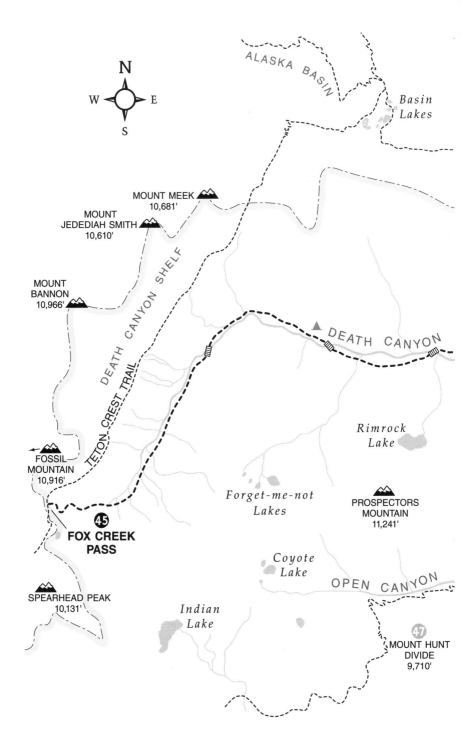

N
W   E
S

ALASKA BASIN

Basin
Lakes

MOUNT MEEK
10,681'

MOUNT
JEDEDIAH SMITH
10,610'

DEATH CANYON SHELF

MOUNT
BANNON
10,966'

DEATH CANYON

TETON CREST TRAIL

Rimrock
Lake

FOSSIL
MOUNTAIN
10,916'

Forget-me-not
Lakes

PROSPECTORS
MOUNTAIN
11,241'

45
FOX CREEK
PASS

Coyote
Lake

OPEN CANYON

SPEARHEAD PEAK
10,131'

Indian
Lake

47
MOUNT HUNT
DIVIDE
9,710'

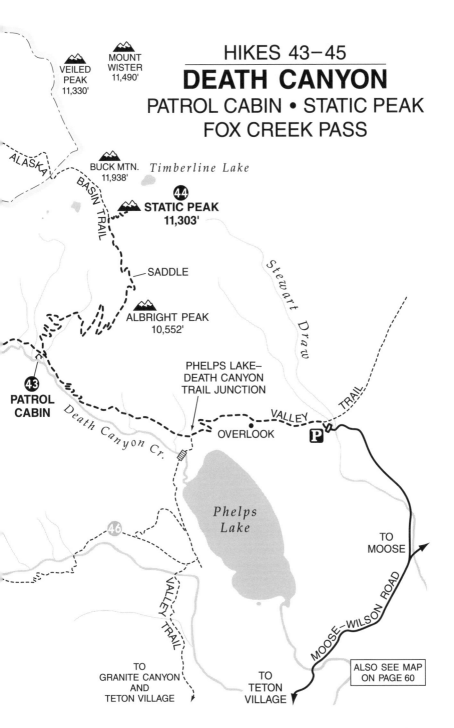

VEILED PEAK 11,330'

MOUNT WISTER 11,490'

ALASKA

BUCK MTN. 11,938'

BASIN TRAIL

Timberline Lake

44
STATIC PEAK
11,303'

SADDLE

ALBRIGHT PEAK 10,552'

Stewart Draw

43
PATROL CABIN

Death Canyon Cr.

PHELPS LAKE–
DEATH CANYON
TRAIL JUNCTION

OVERLOOK

VALLEY

TRAIL

P

Phelps Lake

46

VALLEY TRAIL

TO MOOSE

MOOSE–WILSON ROAD

TO GRANITE CANYON AND TETON VILLAGE

TO TETON VILLAGE

TO TETON VILLAGE

ALSO SEE MAP ON PAGE 60

Hike 46
Open Canyon to the
Open Canyon Creek Bridge

Hiking distance: 8.2 miles round trip
Hiking time: 4 hours
Elevation gain: 1,200 feet
Maps: U.S.G.S. Grand Teton
  Trails Illustrated Grand Teton National Park

Summary of hike: Open Canyon rests between Death Canyon and Granite Canyon along the Teton front range. It is a shallow canyon in relation to the other Teton canyons. Open Canyon is a V-shaped canyon formed by water erosion rather than the typical U-shaped canyons formed by moving glacial ice. The lightly used Open Canyon Trail, due west of Phelps Lake, climbs 4.7 miles up the canyon to the Mount Hunt Divide at 9,710 feet. The trail then heads down the slope to join with the Granite Canyon Trail. This hike, less strenuous than Hike 47, curves around the north end of Phelps Lake and heads up Open Canyon to the Open Canyon Creek bridge.

Driving directions: Same as Hike 42.

Hiking directions: Follow the hiking directions to Phelps Lake and the Death Canyon Trail junction at 1.6 miles (Hike 42). From the posted junction, the right fork leads up Death Canyon (Hikes 43—45). Take the Valley Trail to the left, and cross a bridge over Death Canyon Creek. Ascend the wooded moraine above the expansive west side of Phelps Lake. Follow the base of the Teton Range to a posted junction at 2.6 miles. Leave the Valley Trail and bear right on the Open Canyon Trail. Climb through the woodland, then on the open slopes of Prospectors Mountain. Angle left into Open Canyon to a junction. Go to the right and traverse the stream-fed canyon bottom. Pass through a meadow and cross a bridge over Open Canyon Creek at just over 4 miles. The bridge is our turnaround spot.

To hike further, continue with Hike 47 to Mount Hunt Divide.

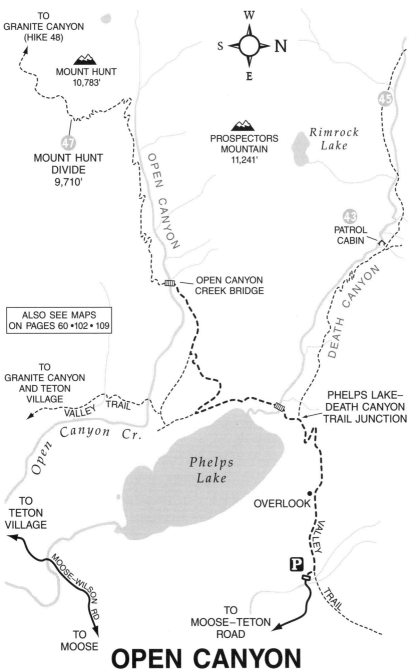

TO
GRANITE CANYON
(HIKE 48)

W N
S E

MOUNT HUNT
10,783'

Rimrock Lake

PROSPECTORS
MOUNTAIN
11,241'

47 MOUNT HUNT
DIVIDE
9,710'

O P E N   C A N Y O N

PATROL
CABIN

45

43

OPEN CANYON
CREEK BRIDGE

D E A T H   C A N Y O N

ALSO SEE MAPS
ON PAGES 60 •102 • 109

TO
GRANITE CANYON
AND TETON
VILLAGE

VALLEY TRAIL

Open Canyon Cr.

PHELPS LAKE–
DEATH CANYON
TRAIL JUNCTION

Phelps Lake

TO
TETON
VILLAGE

OVERLOOK

VALLEY

MOOSE–WILSON RD.

P

TRAIL

TO
MOOSE

TO
MOOSE–TETON
ROAD

OPEN CANYON
TO THE OPEN CANYON CREEK BRIDGE

Hike 47
Open Canyon to Mount Hunt Divide

Hiking distance: 14.6 miles round trip
Hiking time: 7.5 hours
Elevation gain: 3,000 feet
Maps: U.S.G.S. Grand Teton
       Trails Illustrated Grand Teton National Park

map
next page

Summary of hike: Mount Hunt Divide sits at the base of Mount Hunt between Prospectors Mountain and Apres Vous Peak. From the stark, jagged terrain at the summit are magnificent top-of-the-world views of the southern Teton Range, including the predominant Rendezvous Mountain and Apres Vous Peak to the south (the back side of the Jackson Hole Ski Resort), Prospectors Mountain and the major Teton Peaks to the north, and the Gros Ventre Range far to the east. From the Open Canyon Creek bridge (Hike 46), the trail parallels the creek, then steeply zigzags up the south side of the canyon through spruce, fir, and pines to Mount Hunt Divide.

Driving directions: Same as Hike 42.

Hiking directions: Follow the hiking directions to Phelps Lake (Hike 42) and on to the bridge crossing over Open Canyon creek at 4.1 miles (Hike 46). From the bridge, head up the canyon on the moist, north-facing slope. Traverse the hillside above the creek, climbing through subalpine fir, Douglas fir, lodgepole pine, Engelmann spruce, and across a few avalanche chutes. Emerge from the forest at 6 miles to views of the meadows on the floor of Open Canyon and Phelps Lake far below. Continue up the canyon slope to the northeast flank of Mount Hunt. Turn to the south, and begin the trek from the creek bottom up to the divide. Climb the limestone cliffs on short, steep switchbacks through groves of lodgepole and whitebark pines to the 9,710-foot saddle at Mount Hunt Divide. This is our turnaround spot.

    To extend the hike, the trail descends past Mount Hunt and

intersects with the Granite Canyon Trail (Hike 48). This route can be hiked as a 21-mile loop.

Hike 48
Granite Canyon Trail

Hiking distance: 4 to 12.6 miles round trip
Hiking time: 2 to 6 hours
Elevation gain: 600 to 1,600 feet
Maps: U.S.G.S. Teton Village and Rendezvous Peak
    Trails Illustrated Grand Teton National Park

map next page

Summary of hike: Granite Canyon is a U-shaped, glacier-carved canyon near the south end of the Teton Range. The canyon trail connects with the Teton Crest Trail near Marion Lake and also with the summit of Rendezvous Mountain at the top of the Teton Village aerial tram. The hike can be as short or long as you choose, as entering the canyon for even a short distance is a rewarding hike. The hike begins at the mouth of Granite Canyon and climbs moderately along the cascading watercourse to the upper canyon and high mountain meadows. Near the meadows, the creek branches into three forks by the upper Granite Canyon patrol cabin, a rustic log cabin used primarily by work crews maintaining the trails and by patrolling rangers. There are great views down the canyon. The Granite Canyon Trail can be combined with the Open Canyon Trail (Hike 47) for a 21-mile loop or with Rendezvous Mountain (Hike 50) for a 12.4-mile loop.

Driving directions: From the intersection of Highway 89 and Teton Park Road at Moose Junction, drive a half mile west on Teton Park Road to the town Moose. On the left, across the highway from the Moose Visitor Center, is the Moose-Wilson Road to Teton Village. Turn left and continue 5.9 miles to the signed Granite Canyon parking area on the right.
    From Teton Village, drive 2.1 miles north to the trailhead.

Hiking directions: Take the signed Granite Canyon Trail

west through rolling sagebrush meadows and aspen groves. Cross a wooden bridge over Granite Creek and curve north, following the base of the mountains. Pass several overlooks of Granite Creek to a posted Y-fork at 1.5 miles. The left fork (the Valley Trail) leads 2.4 miles to Teton Village. Take the right fork 0.1 mile to a trail split, crossing a bridge over cascading Granite Creek and a second bridge over a creek channel. To the right, the Valley Trail continues to Phelps Lake. Bear left and curve up Granite Canyon on the north side of the cascading creek, passing large granite boulders. Steadily climb under the towering canyon walls through the forested creek bottom with thick vegetation and talus slopes. Continue climbing the canyon past cascades, views of avalanche chutes across the canyon, and a bridge crossing. As you near the upper meadow at 6.2 miles, cross a bridge over a tributary stream to a posted junction by the Granite Canyon patrol cabin. Bear left on the Rendezvous Mountain Trail, and cross bridges over the North Fork, then Middle Fork of Granite Creek. This is our turnaround spot.

To hike further, there are three options. From the patrol cabin, the Granite Canyon Trail continues up the north fork of the canyon 0.8 miles to the Open Canyon Trail on the right (see Hike 47). Continuing straight on the Granite Canyon Trail leads to the Teton Crest Trail near Marion Lake. To the south, the Rendezvous Mountain Trail heads up to the top of the Teton Village aerial tram on the 10,450-foot summit (Hike 50).

HIKES 47 • 48
OPEN CANYON
TO MOUNT HUNT DIVIDE
GRANITE CANYON TRAIL

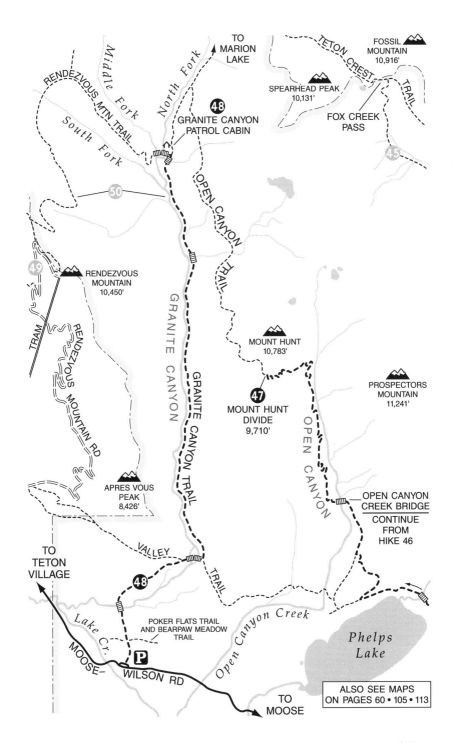

TO
MARION
LAKE

FOSSIL
MOUNTAIN
10,916'

TETON CREST

RENDEZVOUS MTN TRAIL

Middle Fork

North Fork

SPEARHEAD PEAK
10,131'

48
GRANITE CANYON
PATROL CABIN

FOX CREEK
PASS

South Fork

TRAIL

50

OPEN CANYON TRAIL

45

RENDEZVOUS
MOUNTAIN
10,450'

49

GRANITE CANYON

MOUNT HUNT
10,783'

TRAM

RENDEZVOUS MOUNTAIN RD

GRANITE CANYON TRAIL

47
MOUNT HUNT
DIVIDE
9,710'

PROSPECTORS
MOUNTAIN
11,241'

OPEN CANYON

APRES VOUS
PEAK
8,426'

OPEN CANYON
CREEK BRIDGE

CONTINUE
FROM
HIKE 46

TO
TETON
VILLAGE

VALLEY

TRAIL

48

POKER FLATS TRAIL
AND BEARPAW MEADOW
TRAIL

*Phelps
Lake*

Lake Cr.

MOOSE-

P
WILSON RD

Open Canyon Creek

TO
MOOSE

ALSO SEE MAPS
ON PAGES 60 • 105 • 113

Hike 49
Rock Springs Loop—Rendezvous Mountain
JACKSON HOLE SKI RESORT

Hiking distance: 4.2 mile loop
Hiking time: 3 hours
Elevation gain: 1,100 feet
Maps: U.S.G.S. Teton Village and Rendezvous Peak
Rendezvous Mountain Trail Map

**map
next page**

Summary of hike: The Rock Springs Loop trail begins at an elevation of 10,450 feet at the top of the Jackson Hole Ski Resort. The aerial tram at Teton Village runs year round, taking visitors 2.4 miles to the top of Rendezvous Mountain and gaining 4,139 feet en route. The trail traverses across the rugged alpine environment and offers some of the best views of Jackson Hole. Although the weather may be warm down at Teton Village, at this altitude the temperature is cooler and the weather is unpredictable. Bring warm clothing and good shoes.

Driving directions: From Jackson, head south on Highway 89 for 1.3 miles to Highway 22. Turn right and drive 4 miles to Wyoming Highway 390, the Moose-Wilson Road. Turn right and continue 7 miles to Teton Village. Turn left and park in the parking lot by the tram a short distance ahead.

Hiking directions: Take the aerial tram to the top of Rendezvous Mountain. Exit the tram and follow the unpaved road west towards Cody Bowl, a glacial cirque. Pass a trail on the left (our return route) to a posted junction on the right near Cody Bowl. The right fork enters Grand Teton National Park and leads to Marion Lake and Granite Canyon (Hike 50). Continue straight ahead down the switchbacks to the base of Cody Bowl. Take the Rock Springs footpath uphill to the left to another trail split. To the right is a short, optional detour to the Green River Lookout. The Rock Springs Trail on the left continues downhill into a large meadow. From the meadow begins the ascent. At a trail split, take the nature trail, bearing to the right to a junction with the Rendezvous Mountain Road. Take the road to the left, gaining 750 feet as you head back to the tram.

Hike 50
Rendezvous Mountain—Granite Canyon Loop
JACKSON HOLE SKI RESORT

Hiking distance: 12.4 miles round trip
Hiking time: 6 hours
Elevation gain: 4,100 feet

> map
> next page

Maps: U.S.G.S. Rendezvous Peak & Teton Village
      Rendezvous Mountain Trail Map
      Trails Illustrated Grand Teton National Park

Summary of hike: This loop in the Bridger-Teton National Forest connects Rendezvous Mountain with Granite Canyon. It begins at the top of the aerial tram from Teton Village. Starting from the summit, the trail enters Grand Teton National Park and, for the most part, follows a downhill course. The Rendezvous Mountain Trail loops around the upper northwest slope of Rendezvous Mountain, crossing through enormous alpine meadows marbled with small streams and teaming with wildflowers. The trail then drops into Granite Canyon, where there are great views down the rugged canyon. The Granite Canyon Trail descends along the cascading creek through a forest between the steep, towering canyon walls.

Driving directions: Same as Hike 49.

Hiking directions: Take the aerial tram to the top of Rendezvous Mountain. Exit the tram and follow the unpaved road west towards Cody Bowl, a glacial cirque. Pass a trail on the left to a posted junction on the right near Cody Bowl. Bear right on the posted footpath towards Marion Lake and Granite Canyon, entering Grand Teton National Park in a high alpine setting. Head down the hillside and cut back on the switchback to the left. The path curves to the right under a towering vertical cirque. Cross a drainage and ascend the mountainside overlooking Granite Canyon. Top the ridge and descend into a pine forest and then into meadows. Cross over the South Fork Granite Creek to vast open meadows and a posted junction with the Middle Fork Cutoff Trail at 3.5 miles. The left fork leads to Teton Crest and Marion Lake. Stay to the right and descend the open, sloping meadow surrounded by mountains. Pass through pockets of evergreens into forested Granite Canyon. Cross two log footbridges over Granite Creek to the patrol cabin on the left and a posted junction at 5.2 miles. Bear right on the Granite Canyon Trail, and cross a bridge over a tributary stream. Head down the south-facing wall of the canyon, and cross another bridge over a stream below a 100-foot water-fall off the north canyon wall. Continue down canyon, passing rocky beaches to a T-junction at 9.9 miles at the base of the canyon. The left fork leads to Phelps Lake. Bear right and cross two bridges over Granite Creek to a junction a short distance ahead at 10 miles. Take the Valley Trail to the right towards Teton Village. Climb over a small ridge and drop into a valley. Traverse the hillside through aspen groves to a junction at the national park boundary. Leave the park on the right fork, stay-ing on the Valley Trail. Pass the ski maintenance area, and follow the hiking path signs back to the tram.

HIKES 49 • 50
ROCK SPRINGS LOOP
RENDEZVOUS MOUNTAIN– GRANITE CANYON LOOP
JACKSON HOLE SKI RESORT

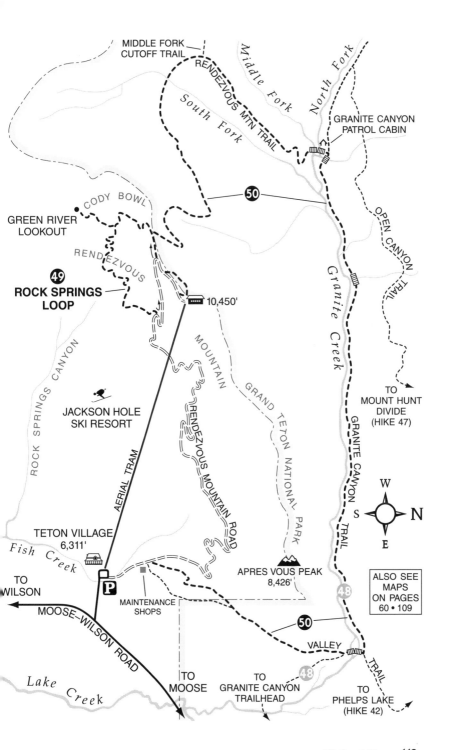

MIDDLE FORK
CUTOFF TRAIL

Middle Fork

North Fork

RENDEZVOUS MTN TRAIL

South Fork

GRANITE CANYON
PATROL CABIN

CODY BOWL

GREEN RIVER
LOOKOUT

50

OPEN CANYON TRAIL

RENDEZVOUS

49
ROCK SPRINGS
LOOP

10,450'

Granite Creek

JACKSON HOLE
SKI RESORT

RENDEZVOUS MOUNTAIN

GRAND TETON NATIONAL PARK

GRANITE CANYON TRAIL

TO
MOUNT HUNT
DIVIDE
(HIKE 47)

ROCK SPRINGS CANYON

AERIAL TRAM

RENDEZVOUS MOUNTAIN ROAD

W

N

S

E

TETON VILLAGE
6,311'

Fish Creek

APRES VOUS PEAK
8,426'

48

ALSO SEE
MAPS
ON PAGES
60 • 109

TO
WILSON

P

MAINTENANCE
SHOPS

MOOSE–WILSON ROAD

50

VALLEY TRAIL

Lake Creek

TO
MOOSE

TO
GRANITE CANYON
TRAILHEAD

48

TO
PHELPS LAKE
(HIKE 42)

Hike 51
Cunningham Cabin

Hiking distance: 0.5 mile loop
Hiking time: 20 minutes
Elevation gain: Level
Maps: U.S.G.S. Moran
            Cunningham Cabin Guide

Summary of hike: Cunningham Cabin was the 160-acre homestead ranch of J. Pierce and Margaret Cunningham from the 1880s. The homestead is located just south of Spread Creek in the flatlands overlooking the Snake River between Moose Junction and Moran Junction. The ranch was primarily used for grazing cattle and cultivating hay. All that remains of the historic homesite are buck-and-rail fences, foundation stones, broken posts, and depressions. The existing cabin, built in the 1950s, is a replica of the original 1880s cabin. The half-mile, self-guiding trail circles the cabin, foundation, and surrounding grounds.

Driving directions: From the intersection of Highway 89 and Teton Park Road at Moose Junction, drive 12.5 miles north on Highway 89 to the posted Cunningham Cabin on the left. Turn left and continue 0.4 miles to the parking lot at the end of the road. (The turnoff to the cabin is 5.3 miles south of Moran Junction.)

Hiking directions: Walk through the buck-and-rail fence, overlooking the expansive flatlands of Jackson Hole and the entire Teton Range. Head northwest through the open grasslands. Curve right and cross a bridge over the creek to the low, three-room cabin with a sod roof. Continue past the cabin, passing depressions and remnants of foundations while sensing the history associated with the area. The trail returns along the rear of the cabin and completes the loop.

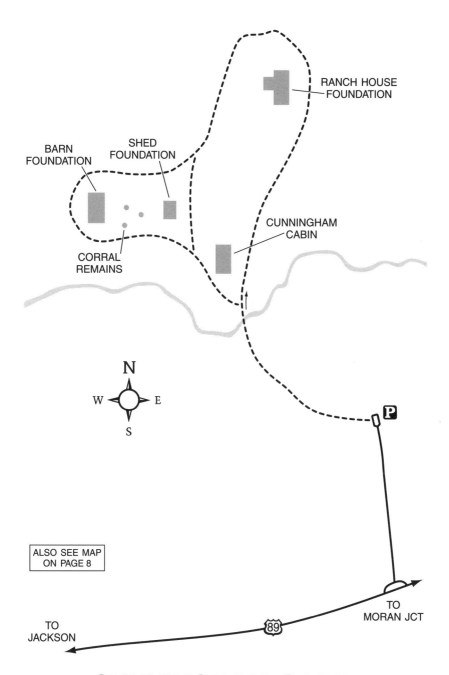

RANCH HOUSE
FOUNDATION

BARN
FOUNDATION

SHED
FOUNDATION

CUNNINGHAM
CABIN

CORRAL
REMAINS

N
W — E
S

ALSO SEE MAP
ON PAGE 8

P

TO
MORAN JCT

89

TO
JACKSON

CUNNINGHAM CABIN

Hike 52
Schwabacher's Landing

Hiking distance: 1 to 4 miles round trip
Hiking time: 30 minutes to 2 hours
Elevation gain: Level
Maps: U.S.G.S. Moose

Summary of hike: Schwabacher's Landing is a launch site on the Snake River between Moose Junction and Moran Junction, popular with anglers and river rafters. This flat river area is home to moose, elk, deer, antelope, coyote, beaver, otter, eagles, and abundant waterfowl. The trail meanders along the banks of the Snake River past beaver dams and partially chewed trees. Throughout the hike are picturesque views of the Tetons and their reflection in the water.

Driving directions: From the intersection of Highway 89 and Teton Park Road at Moose Junction, drive 4 miles north to Schwabacher Landing Road on the left. (The turnoff is 16.3 miles north of downtown Jackson.) Turn left onto the gravel road, and continue 0.6 miles to a road split. The left fork leads 0.1 mile to a parking area. The right fork leads 0.4 miles further to another parking area.

Hiking directions: From either parking area, the unmaintained network of trails is well defined. Used by animals and people, the trails follow along the riverbank and side channels of the Snake River through a forest of cottonwood and willow trees. With the river to the west and the highway and sagebrush flats to the east, you may easily wander upstream or downstream without getting lost.

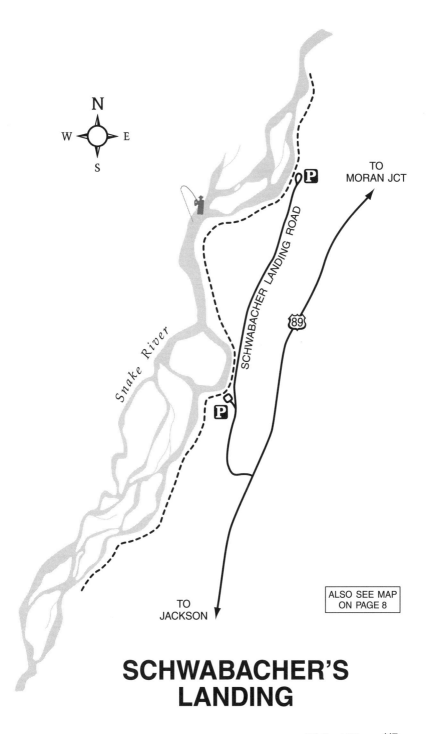

N
W   E
S

P

TO
MORAN JCT

SCHWABACHER LANDING ROAD

89

Snake River

P

TO
JACKSON

ALSO SEE MAP
ON PAGE 8

SCHWABACHER'S
LANDING

Hike 53
Blacktail Butte—North Access

Hiking distance: 4 miles round trip
Hiking time: 2.5 hours
Elevation gain: 1,100 feet
Maps: U.S.G.S. Moose

map
next page

Summary of hike: Blacktail Butte is a prominent 7,688-foot butte that stands alone at the south end of Antelope Flats near Moose Junction. Glaciers flowing down the valley sculpted the oval-shaped form of this Madison limestone butte. Rising 1,100 feet above the valley floor, the butte extends nearly three miles north and south along Highway 89 and is two miles wide. Blacktail Butte has trailheads at both the north end by Moose Junction (Hike 53) and on the southeast side near Gros Ventre Road (Hike 54). Both trails connect at the summit, where there are sweeping vistas of the surrounding landscape. To the north and west are views across the Jackson Hole valley to the Teton Range. To the south and east are views across the National Elk Refuge to the Gros Ventre Range. Hikes 53 and 54 may be combined for a 4.8-mile, one-way shuttle hike.

Driving directions: From the intersection of Highway 89 and Teton Park Road at Moose Junction, drive 0.9 miles north on Highway 89 to the Blacktail Butte parking lot on the right.

Hiking directions: Take the path on the right, and head south along the base of Blacktail Butte through a mix of pines, aspens, and sagebrush. At 0.3 miles, the trail curves left, following the contour of the mountain. Walk through open grasslands and aspen groves to the mouth of the wooded canyon. Enter the canyon and hop over to the east side of the stream. Cross a talus slope and walk beneath an overhanging rock wall and huge outcroppings. Steadily climb the wooded drainage on the west-facing hillside to an open, sloping meadow colored with wildflowers. At the top, south end of the meadow, reenter the forest. Wind through the forest on a gentle grade. After a short, steep ascent, the path emerges from the forest to a sage-covered slope. Climb the slope to incredible views of the majestic Teton Range to the northwest. Make a sharp left bend, and head 40 yards uphill to a junction at the ridge. Take the spur trail 25 yards to the right to the 7,688-foot summit. This is our turnaround spot.

Hike 54
Blacktail Butte—East Access

Hiking distance: 5.6 miles round trip
Hiking time: 3 hours
Elevation gain: 1,100 feet
Maps: U.S.G.S. Gros Ventre Junction and Moose
Trails Illustrated Grand Teton National Park

map
next page

Summary of hike: Same as Hike 53.

Driving directions: From downtown Jackson, drive 6.5 miles north on Highway 89 towards Grand Teton National Park to the Gros Ventre Junction. (The junction is located 5.5 miles south of Moose Junction.) Turn right and continue 5 miles to Mormon Row, a wide, unsigned road on the left. The road is located 0.4 miles past the Gros Ventre Campground. Turn left and drive 0.4 miles on the unpaved road to the metal gate on the left. Park off road without blocking the gate.

Hiking directions: Walk west on the vehicle-restricted dirt road, heading across the sage-covered flat to the base of Blacktail Butte. Climb a small rise dotted with aspens. Just before reaching the top of the slope, a narrow footpath veers off to the right. Take this path and steeply climb the 500-foot ridge of the barren, east-facing slope. At the ridgetop are sweeping vistas from the Jackson Hole valley to the town of Jackson. Traverse the rolling ridge between the forested north slope and the sage-covered south slope. Cross a saddle and curve to the right, passing through a small pocket of fir trees. Continue climbing on the open slope, traversing the hillside to a saddle at the head of the draw. Walk through a meadow with a round, crater-shaped pond, then wind through Douglas fir and lodgepole pine groves while looping around to the left. Ascend the open slope as the trail fades. Just before reaching the top of the knoll, an unsigned path bears left. Take this path a short distance to a ridge with a spur trail on the left. Head up this path 25 yards to the 7,688-foot summit. This is our turn-around spot. After enjoying the views, return on the same trail.

This hike can be combined with Hike 53 for a 4.8-mile, one-way shuttle hike.

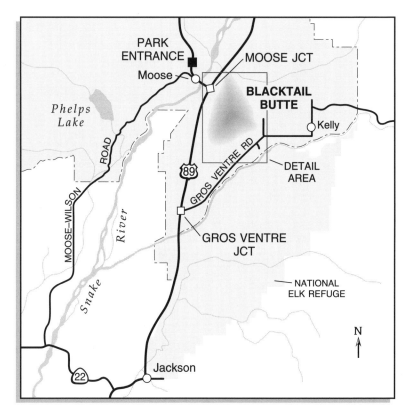

HIKES 53 • 54
BLACKTAIL BUTTE
NORTH ACCESS • EAST ACCESS

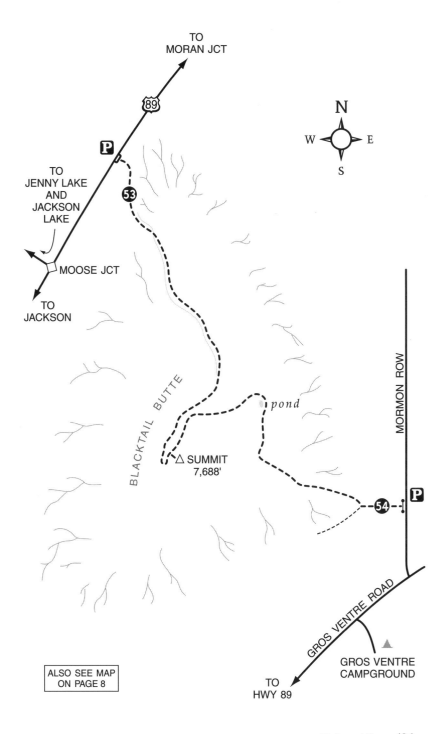

TO
MORAN JCT

(89)

N
W ✦ E
S

P

TO
JENNY LAKE
AND
JACKSON
LAKE

53

MOOSE JCT

TO
JACKSON

BLACKTAIL BUTTE

MORMON ROW

pond

△ SUMMIT
7,688'

54 **P**

GROS VENTRE ROAD

ALSO SEE MAP
ON PAGE 8

TO
HWY 89

GROS VENTRE
CAMPGROUND

Hike 55
Lower Slide Lake
GROS VENTRE SLIDE INTERPRETIVE TRAIL

Hiking distance: 1.2 miles round trip
Hiking time: 1 hour
Elevation gain: 200 feet
Maps: U.S.G.S. Shadow Mountain
Earthwalk Press: Grand Teton National Park, Wyoming

Summary of hike: The Gros Ventre River, a tributary of the Snake River, winds into Jackson Hole through Antelope Flats, forming a portion of the southern boundary of Grand Teton National Park. On June 23, 1925, a 2,000-foot avalanche from Sheep Mountain, on the south side of the river valley, blocked the canyon and formed a natural dam 225-feet high and a mile wide. The dam blocked the Gros Ventre River, creating Lower Slide Lake. The three-mile lake is now a popular recreation site. The Gros Ventre Slide Interpretive Trail is a 0.8-mile hike along a self-guided nature trail. The trail overlooks the largest natural landslide of historical record in North America. Informative signs along the trail discuss the geology and flora of the area.

Driving directions: From Jackson, drive 6.5 miles north on Highway 89 to the Gros Ventre Junction. Turn right on Gros Ventre Road, and drive 8 miles to the T-intersection where Gros Ventre Road heads to the right. Turn right and drive 4.7 miles to the trailhead. The parking turnout is on the right.

Hiking directions: Follow the trail southeast from the parking area. As you hike down the hill, other trail options appear. They all weave around and reconnect with the main loop. Benches are provided throughout the hike. The fisherman trails that lead beyond the interpretive trail to Lower Slide Lake are worth exploring. Return along the same route back to the parking area.

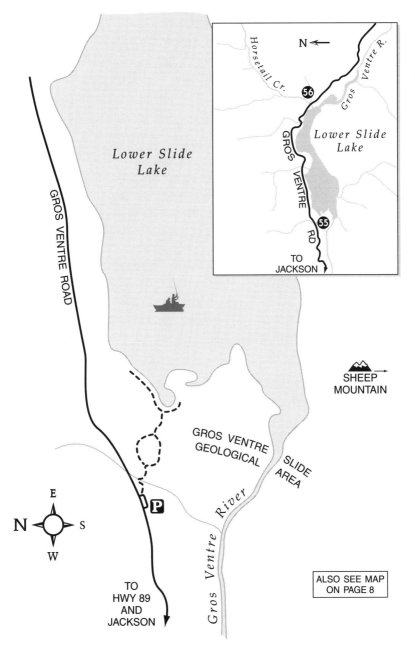

Lower Slide Lake

Horsetail Cr.

Gros Ventre R.

56

Lower Slide Lake

GROS VENTRE

55

RD

TO JACKSON

N ←

GROS VENTRE ROAD

SHEEP MOUNTAIN

GROS VENTRE GEOLOGICAL

SLIDE AREA

Gros Ventre River

P

E
N — S
W

TO HWY 89 AND JACKSON

ALSO SEE MAP ON PAGE 8

LOWER SLIDE LAKE
GROS VENTRE SLIDE INTERPRETIVE TRAIL

Hike 56
Horsetail Creek Trail

Hiking distance: 3.4 miles round trip
Hiking time: 1.5 hours
Elevation gain: 600 feet
Maps: U.S.G.S. Mount Leidy
              Trails Illustrated Grand Teton National Park

Summary of hike: The Horsetail Creek Trail in the Gros Ventre Mountains is a quiet, lightly used trail that winds through a beautiful forest. The trail parallels and crosses Horsetail Creek through rolling hills with meadows, canyons, and streams.

Driving directions: From Jackson, drive 6.5 miles north on Highway 89 to the Gros Ventre Junction. Turn right on Gros Ventre Road, and drive 8 miles to the T-intersection where Gros Ventre Road heads to the right. Turn right and continue 7.6 miles to the Horsetail Creek Trailhead parking area on the left. The trailhead is located immediately after the road crosses Horsetail Creek.

Hiking directions: From the parking area, hike north past the trailhead sign and into the draw. Rock hop across the stream. At 0.3 miles, the trail crosses Horsetail Creek. Just before reaching the creek, a footpath to the right leads to a log crossing. After crossing, return to the main trail. Continue up the canyon to a trail split at 0.8 miles. The right fork crosses Horsetail Creek and leads a short distance into a lush, narrow canyon. Return to the junction and continue on the left fork up a ridge to a fence and gate. Once past the gate, the gradient steepens, gaining 400 feet in the next 0.6 miles. As the trail levels off, it nears the creek and crosses a tributary stream to another trail split. This is our turnaround spot. Return by retracing your steps.

To hike further, the trail crosses a divide and continues along the Middle Fork of Ditch Creek to a junction with the North Fork and Main Fork of Ditch Creek. The right fork follows the North

Fork Ditch Creek into the Mount Leidy Highlands. The left fork follows Ditch Creek to the Teton Science School, north of Kelly.

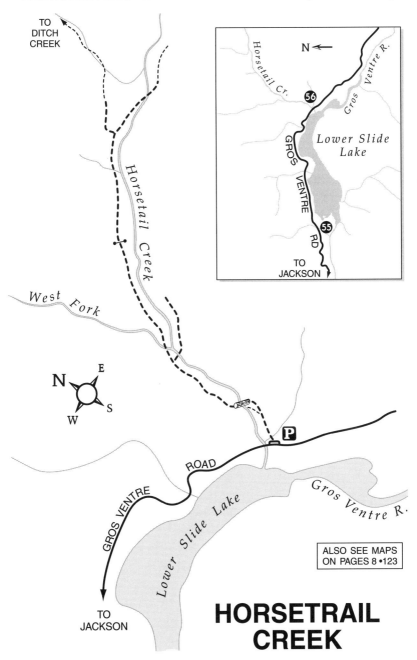

ALSO SEE MAPS
ON PAGES 8 •123

HORSETRAIL CREEK

Hike 57
Lower Sheep Creek Canyon

Hiking distance: 3 miles round trip
Hiking time: 1.5 hours
Elevation gain: 1,000 feet
Maps: U.S.G.S. Gros Ventre Junction

Summary of hike: Lower Sheep Creek Canyon lies near the east end of the National Elk Refuge in the Teton National Forest. The access trail begins in the refuge and quickly enters the mouth of the canyon. The hike leads to two overlooks located on the west slope of the Gros Ventre Range. From the overlooks, perched 600 feet above the valley floor, are expansive views across the elk refuge, the Teton Range, the Snake River Range, Jackson Peak, and into Sheep Creek Canyon.

Driving directions: From downtown Jackson, drive east on Broadway (the main street through Jackson) 0.9 miles to the end of Broadway. Turn left into the National Elk Refuge. Drive 6 miles towards the Curtis Canyon Campground, following the signs. The trailhead is on the left by the Teton National Forest boundary sign, just before winding up the mountain to the campground.

Hiking directions: Take the wide path across the open sage flats on the east end of the National Elk Refuge. Follow the west edge of the hillside 100 yards to the mouth of the canyon and a trail split. The left fork crosses the aspen-lined creek and zig-zags up the north canyon wall to an overlook of the elk preserve, the town of Jackson, and the Teton Range. Return to the trail split, and take the right fork (now on your left), staying in the canyon under the shade of pines and fir. The trail parallels the south side of Sheep Creek through the narrow canyon, steadily gaining elevation. The undulating path climbs the canyon wall to open meadows and returns to the creek in the shaded woodland. Pass a stream-fed side canyon across the creek on the vertical north canyon wall. A short distance ahead, the trail ends at the creek. A faint path heads up the canyon wall to the right. The steep climb ends at the Curtis Canyon Viewpoint by Curtis Campground. While climbing the hillside, the trail fades in and out, so when in doubt, curve to the right. For a loop hike with sweeping vistas, descend on the unpaved road. The trailhead is at the base of the hill.

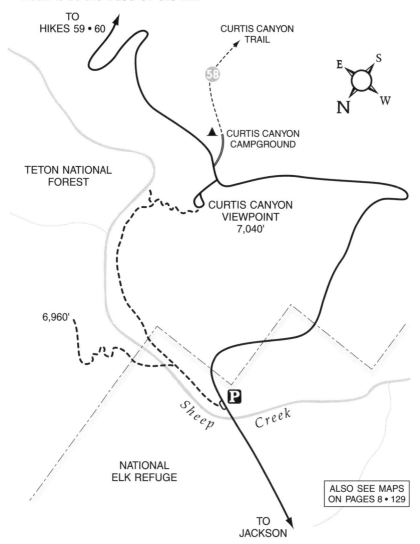

LOWER SHEEP CREEK CANYON

Hike 58
Curtis Canyon Trail

Hiking distance: 3 miles round trip
Hiking time: 1.5 hours
Elevation gain: 700 feet
Maps: U.S.G.S. Gros Ventre Junction
        Earthwalk Press: Grand Teton National Park, Wyoming

Summary of hike: The Curtis Canyon Trail is an old ranch road reclaimed by the grassy meadow. The two-track trail begins at the Curtis Canyon Campground and heads downhill through a narrow canyon parallel to North Twin Creek. There are four creek crossings and magnificent rock formations.

Driving directions: From downtown Jackson, drive east on Broadway (the main street through Jackson) 0.9 miles to the end of Broadway. Turn left into the National Elk Refuge, and drive 7.1 miles to the signed Curtis Canyon Viewpoint. Park on the left.

Hiking directions: Head 30 yards up the road to the Curtis Canyon Campground on the right. Follow the road through the campground 0.2 miles to the far south end of the loop by campsite 10. Several unsigned paths leave the campground and join the easily seen main trail in the meadow. The two-track trail heads south down the draw fringed with conifers. Descend into the canyon along North Twin Creek. To the right are steep cliffs with sculpted rock formations. At 0.7 miles, cross the creek and continue down the narrow canyon in the shade of the forest. Follow the watercourse through the forest, recrossing the creek at one mile. At the mouth of the canyon, cross the creek again, then emerge to wonderful views of the Tetons. At 1.6 miles the trail crosses South Twin Creek at an unpaved private road at the Twin Creek Ranch boundary. To return, hike back up the canyon along the same trail.

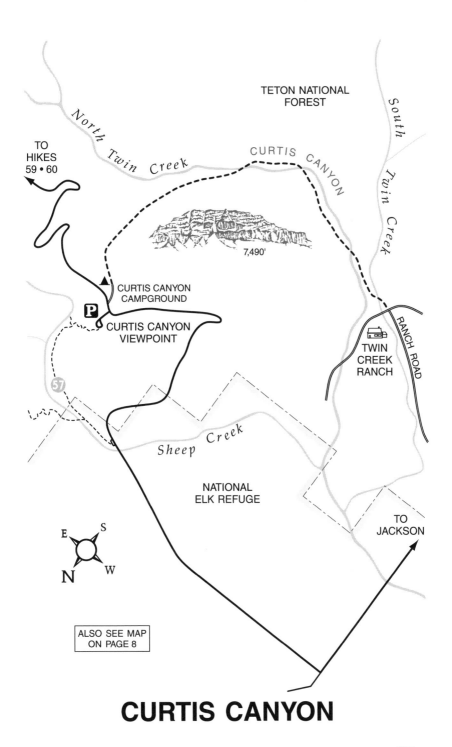

TETON NATIONAL
FOREST

North Twin Creek

South Twin Creek

CURTIS CANYON

TO
HIKES
59 • 60

7,490'

▲ CURTIS CANYON
CAMPGROUND

P

CURTIS CANYON
VIEWPOINT

RANCH ROAD

TWIN
CREEK
RANCH

57

Sheep Creek

NATIONAL
ELK REFUGE

TO
JACKSON

E · S · N · W

ALSO SEE MAP
ON PAGE 8

CURTIS CANYON

Hike 59
Goodwin Lake

Hiking distance: 6 miles round trip
Hiking time: 3 hours
Elevation gain: 1,500 feet
Maps: U.S.G.S. Gros Ventre Junction, Blue Miner Lake,
    and Turquoise Lake
    Trails Illustrated Grand Teton National Park

map
next page

Summary of hike: Goodwin Lake sits in a glacial cirque on the east flank of the prominent, cone-shaped Jackson Peak. The small timberline lake in the Gros Ventre Wilderness is rimmed with whitebark pine and Engelmann spruce on the north, east, and south shores. The steep talus slopes of Jackson Peak rise from the western shoreline. The trail to Goodwin Lake follows a narrow 9,000-foot ridge through open forests, high above Sheep Creek Canyon, to the north end of the lake at the base of Jackson Peak.

Driving directions: From downtown Jackson, drive east on Broadway (the main street through Jackson) 0.9 miles to the end of Broadway. Turn left into the National Elk Refuge. Drive towards the Curtis Canyon Campground, following the signs. At 6 miles, the road leaves the flatlands and enters the Teton National Forest. Wind 3 miles up the mountain, passing the campground, to a road split. The Sheep Creek Road bears left (Hike 60). Take the right fork one mile towards Goodwin Lake to the trailhead on the left at the end of the road.

Hiking directions: Pass the trailhead sign and climb through grassy meadows and open pine forest. Views of the elk preserve, the Teton peaks, and barren Jackson Peak tower above the forest. Near the top of the slope, curve to the right and head south. Follow the narrow, forested ridge above Sheep Creek Canyon on the left and the Twin Creek drainage on the right. At 2.2 miles, the trail enters the Gros Ventre Wilderness. Leave the narrow ridge 30 yards ahead, and traverse the east-facing cliffs perched high above Sheep Creek Canyon. Climb through the forest on the root- and rock-strewn path to the outlet stream of Goodwin Lake by a trail sign. Cross the creek to the left, and parallel the creek's east bank to the north end of the lake. The trail continues along the east side of the lake, passes Jackson Peak, and connects with the Cache Creek Trail (Hike 61). A path circles the lake, but a portion of the trail on the west side crosses a steep talus slope along the base of Jackson Peak. Return along the same trail.

Hike 60
Upper Sheep Creek Canyon

Hiking distance: 2.5 miles round trip
Hiking time: 1.5 hours
Elevation gain: 200 feet
Maps: U.S.G.S. Blue Miner Lake and Turquoise Lake
        Trails Illustrated Grand Teton National Park

map
next page

Summary of hike: Sheep Creek Canyon is located in the Gros Ventre Range between the 400-foot high ridge to Goodwin Lake on the west (Hike 59) and Table Mountain on the east. The stream-fed canyon flows through a beautifully forested grassland meadow with pine groves and wildflowers. The isolated trail follows the east ridge of the canyon down to the creek.

Driving directions: From downtown Jackson, drive east on Broadway (the main street through Jackson) 0.9 miles to the end of Broadway. Turn left into the National Elk Refuge. Drive towards the Curtis Canyon Campground, following the signs. At 6 miles, the road leaves the flatlands and enters the Teton National Forest. Wind 3 miles up the mountain, passing the campground, to a road split. The road to Goodwin Lake curves to the right (Hike 59). Take the Sheep Creek Road to the left, and drive 2.4 miles to an old jeep road veering off to the right. This is the trailhead. Park off the road.

Hiking directions: Walk up the old jeep road through open

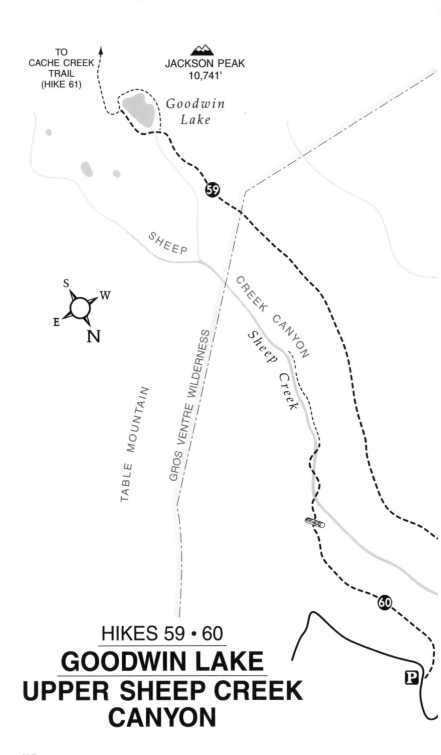

TO
CACHE CREEK
TRAIL
(HIKE 61)

JACKSON PEAK
10,741'

*Goodwin
Lake*

59

SHEEP

CREEK CANYON

Sheep Creek

GROS VENTRE WILDERNESS

TABLE MOUNTAIN

S W
E N

60

P

HIKES 59 • 60
GOODWIN LAKE
UPPER SHEEP CREEK
CANYON

brush and a mixed conifer forest. Gently climb to a ridge over-looking Sheep Creek Canyon; Jackson Peak, which looms over the canyon; and the Teton peaks in the distance. The ridge across the valley is the route to Goodwin Lake (Hike 59). Traverse the east edge of the canyon, gradually descending into the forest. The old jeep road ends at one mile in a mead-ow at the valley floor. Cross over a log barrier to a footpath leading to Sheep Creek. At the creek are open grasslands teeming with wildflowers and rimmed with pines. Meander through the riparian vegetation and pastoral surroundings. An old trail continues up the canyon, but it is not maintained and has become overgrown and difficult to follow. Return along the same trail.

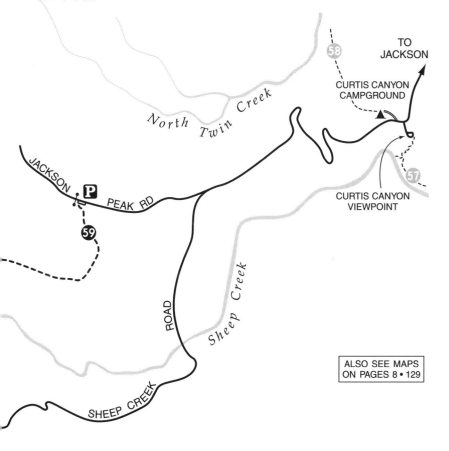

TO
JACKSON

CURTIS CANYON
CAMPGROUND

North Twin Creek

JACKSON PEAK RD

CURTIS CANYON
VIEWPOINT

59

Sheep Creek

ROAD

Sheep Creek

SHEEP CREEK

ALSO SEE MAPS
ON PAGES 8 • 129

Hike 61
Cache Creek Canyon Loop

Hiking distance: 4 miles round trip
Hiking time: 2 hours
Elevation gain: 350 feet
Maps: U.S.G.S. Cache Creek
           Greater Snow King Area Trail Map

Summary of hike: The Cache Creek Trail, part of the Greater Snow King Trail Network, is located on the east edge of Jackson, close to downtown. The trailhead is at the mouth of the canyon in the Gros Ventre Range and skirts the outer edge of the Gros Ventre Wilderness. This popular hiking, biking, and cross-country ski trail weaves through the forest alongside Cache Creek and connects with other trails deep in the wooded backcountry. This loop hike follows the first 2 miles of the trail on each side of the creek. The hike can be combined with the Game Creek Trail (Hike 69) for a 11.7-mile one-way shuttle.

Driving directions: From downtown Jackson, drive east on Broadway (the main street through Jackson) for a half mile to Redmond Street, across from St. John's Hospital. Turn right and drive 0.4 miles to Cache Creek Drive. Turn left and continue 1.2 miles to the parking lot at the end of the road.

Hiking directions: Walk 50 yards back down the entrance road to the bridge crossing Cache Creek on the left. Cross the bridge to a streamside path on the left 40 yards ahead. This narrow side path fades out at the south bank of the creek. Continue on the main path another 40 yards to a 3-way split. The two right forks head up the hillside and lead up Snow King Mountain. Take the left fork and traverse the hillside above Cache Creek. The path parallels the southwest side of Cache Creek, heading upstream. At one mile, there is the option of crossing the stream at a log crossing and returning on the jeep trail or continuing on the same trail farther into the valley. At two miles, there is a Y-fork in the trail. The right fork continues deeper into the canyon and connects to Goodwin Lake (Hike 59), Game Creek (Hike 69), and Granite Falls (Hike 72). To combine this hike with the Game Creek Trail for a one-way shuttle, continue up canyon to the posted junction on the right at 3.8 miles. To return to the trailhead, take the left fork and cross the creek. If you wish to stay dry, there are down logs in both directions of this crossing that can be carefully used as a bridge. After the stream crossing, follow the trail through a meadow to the jeep trail, which heads gently downhill back to the trailhead.

TO GAME CREEK AND GRANITE FALLS (HIKES 69 • 72)

SALT LICK DRAW

JACKSON PEAK 10,741'

PUTT-PUTT TRAIL

GROS VENTRE RANGE

WOODS CANYON

62

GROS VENTRE WILDERNESS

E
N — S
W

P

P

TO SNOW KING MOUNTAIN

CACHE CREEK DR.

Cache Creek

TO HIKES 57–60

NATIONAL ELK REFUGE

NELSON

REDMOND

HOSPITAL

BROADWAY AVE

Cache Creek

ALSO SEE MAPS ON PAGES 8 • 137 • 151

89

Jackson

TO GRAND TETON NAT'L. PARK

Flat Creek

CACHE CREEK CANYON

Hike 62
Woods Canyon

Hiking distance: 2 miles round trip
Hiking time: 1 hour
Elevation gain: 580 feet
Maps: U.S.G.S. Cache Creek

Summary of hike: Woods Canyon is a narrow side canyon that heads north from the mouth of Cache Creek Canyon in the Gros Ventre Range. The area is popular for mountain biking, but the Woods Canyon Trail is open to foot and horse traffic only. The trail winds up a narrow, stream-fed canyon in the Gros Ventre Wilderness.

Driving directions: From downtown Jackson, drive east on Broadway (the main street through Jackson) for a half mile to Redmond Street, across from St. John's Hospital. Turn right and drive 0.4 miles to Cache Creek Drive. Turn left and continue 1.2 miles to the parking lot at the end of the road.

Hiking directions: From the main parking area, walk 100 yards back down the entrance road to the bridge on the left crossing Cache Creek (Hike 61). Take the opposite path across the road on the right. Pass through a pole fence, and climb a short knoll to a junction. The left fork returns to a parking area on Cache Creek Road. Bear right and wind through aspen groves and a lush understory of vegetation to a posted junction with the Putt-Putt Trail on the left, a popular mountain biking trail along the base of the Gros Ventre Mountains. Continue 30 yards straight ahead to another junction. The Putt-Putt Trail curves right. Take the footpath left, heading into Woods Canyon to a posted trail split. The left fork is a connector trail to Nelson Drive. Stay to the right into the narrowing canyon, entering the Gros Ventre Wilderness. Continue up the canyon floor. As the trail curves north, the grade gets steep, crossing talus slopes between towering rock formations. This is our turnaround spot. Return by retracing your steps.

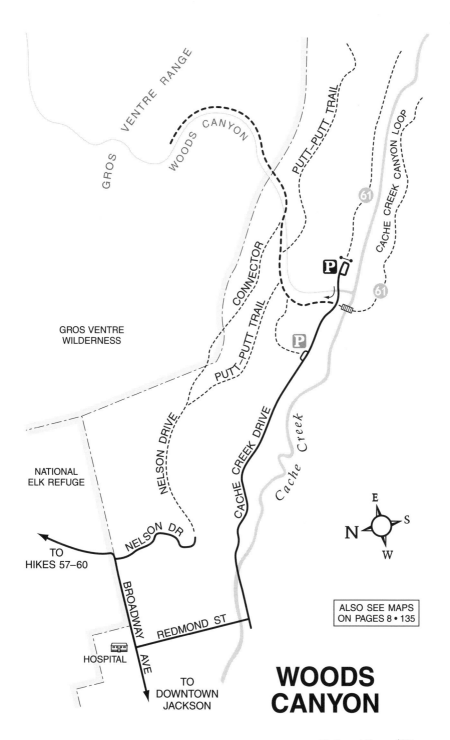

GROS VENTRE RANGE

WOODS CANYON

PUTT-PUTT TRAIL

GROS

CACHE CREEK CANYON LOOP

61

61

CONNECTOR

GROS VENTRE
WILDERNESS

P

P

PUTT-PUTT TRAIL

NELSON DRIVE

CACHE CREEK DRIVE

Cache Creek

NATIONAL
ELK REFUGE

NELSON DR

E

S

N

W

TO
HIKES 57–60

BROADWAY

REDMOND ST

AVE

ALSO SEE MAPS
ON PAGES 8 • 135

HOSPITAL

TO
DOWNTOWN
JACKSON

WOODS
CANYON

Hike 63
Snake River Northeast Dike

Hiking distance: 3 miles round trip
Hiking time: 1.5 hours
Elevation gain: Level
Maps: U.S.G.S. Jackson and Teton Village

Summary of hike: The Snake River Northeast Dike follows the Snake River upstream along a road closed to vehicles. The dikes were built by the Army Corps of Engineers beginning in the 1950s to stop the flooding and erosion of adjacent pasturelands. The man-made rock and dirt berms border both sides of the Snake River from the airport to South Park. The levee is a popular year-around hiking, biking, and cross country ski route that is also perfect for dogs, especially those that love the water. The hike begins at Emily's Pond, an eleven-acre public park donated by Emily Stevens as a preserved habitat for moose, deer, and waterfowl.

Driving directions: From Jackson, head south on Highway 89 for 1.3 miles to Highway 22. Turn right and drive 3.6 miles towards Wilson. Turn right just before crossing the bridge over the Snake River. Park on the right in Emily's Pond parking lot.

Hiking directions: Take the paved road past the ponds on the right to the Snake River. Follow the wide gravel road, heading upstream along the dike. The path crosses the lush wetlands. There is no shade along the dike, but side paths lead through the cottonwood and blue spruce forests to the Snake River on the left and the ponds on the right. At 1.5 miles, the trail ends at a locked gate. Return by reversing your route.

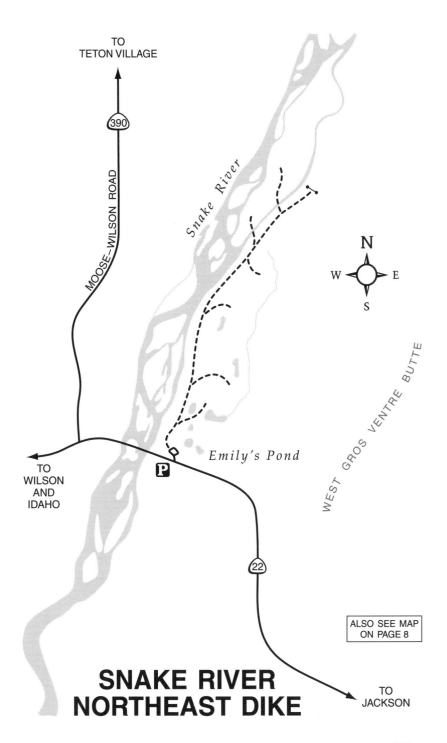

TO
TETON VILLAGE

390

MOOSE–WILSON ROAD

Snake River

N
W E
S

TO
WILSON
AND
IDAHO

P

Emily's Pond

WEST GROS VENTRE BUTTE

22

ALSO SEE MAP
ON PAGE 8

SNAKE RIVER
NORTHEAST DIKE

TO
JACKSON

Hike 64
Teton Pass Trail
OLD PASS ROAD TO CRATER LAKE

Hiking distance: 2.5 miles round trip
Hiking time: 1.5 hours
Elevation gain: 700 feet
Maps: U.S.G.S. Teton Pass
       Trails Illustrated Grand Teton National Park

Summary of hike: The Teton Pass Trail sits on the east side of Teton Pass beneath the towering 10,000-foot twin peaks of Mount Glory. An avalanche chute on Mount Glory, named Glory Slide, dammed the North Fork Trail Creek in 1932. The dam formed Crater Lake, a beautiful lake tucked into the mountains. This loop hike parallels Trail Creek to Crater Lake and returns on the Old Pass Road, the abandoned highway closed in 1970 when the present Highway 22 was completed. The trail winds through a pristine area with an array of wildflowers. In the winter, the Old Pass Road is used as a cross-country ski trail.

Driving directions: From Jackson, head south on Highway 89 for 1.3 miles to Highway 22. Turn right and drive 1.4 miles to Wilson. Continue 1.2 miles past Wilson to a building on the right side of the road with a large sign that says "Heidelberg." Turn left across the highway from this sign. Drive one mile to the gate across Old Pass Road and park.

Hiking directions: Walk around the trail gate, and follow the old asphalt road for 300 yards to a well-defined footpath on the left. Begin the loop to the left, and descend into the forest, parallel to and below the Old Pass Road. Traverse the south-facing hillside above cascading Trail Creek and beneath Mount Glory, towering over the trail. At one mile, rock-hop over the tumbling North Fork Trail Creek. Continue through the forest on a gentle uphill grade, and cross under power poles. Curve right onto an old gravel road for a short distance to Teton Pass (Hike 67). The left fork continues uphill to the summit. Bear right for 50 yards to the Crater Lake outlet stream. Take the short path on the right (east) side of the outlet creek to an overlook of the lake. Cascading waters from the north fork feed the lake.

Return down the Old Pass Road back to the trailhead.

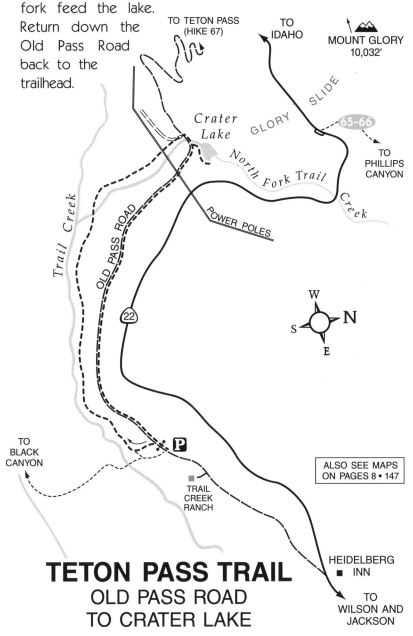

TETON PASS TRAIL
OLD PASS ROAD
TO CRATER LAKE

Hike 65
Phillips Ridge

Hiking distance: 4.4 miles round trip
Hiking time: 2 hours
Elevation gain: 700 feet
Maps: U.S.G.S. Rendezvous Peak
Trails Illustrated Grand Teton National Park

Summary of hike: Phillips Ridge forms the southeast wall of Phillips Canyon at the south end of the Teton Range. The two-mile ridge begins near Teton Pass, west of Jackson, and runs northeast towards Phillips Canyon. The Phillips Ridge Trail follows an unpaved service road through an Engelmann spruce and Douglas fir forest to a fire lookout on the ridge. From the ridge are great views of the valley, the Snake River Range, the Tetons, Rendezvous Peak, and the twin peaks of Mount Glory.

Driving directions: From Jackson, head south on Highway 89 for 1.3 miles to Highway 22. Turn right and drive 1.4 miles to Wilson. Continue 4.1 miles past Wilson to the posted Phillips Canyon trailhead on the right side of the road. On the left side is a parking area. Turn left and park.

Hiking directions: Carefully cross the highway to the signed Phillips Canyon Road and head uphill. Follow the forested road northeast to a signed road fork at 0.4 miles. The left fork leads to Ski Lake (Hike 66) and Phillips Pass. Stay to the right, continuing up the winding road. For a quarter mile, the road parallels the trail to Ski Lake high to the left. At one mile, the trail curves right at a Forest Service sign by a buck fence. Disregard the two-track side roads that intersect the main route. A short distance ahead, the road parallels power lines. At 1.7 miles, the road crosses under the power lines at a road split. At this fork are great views to the west of Mount Glory. Bear to the right, beginning a loop around the ridge. Head up the ridge through stands of aspens. Short side paths lead to overlooks. Follow the ridge east past a fire lookout at the summit. Continue past the lookout, bearing left at a road junction, and complete the loop. Head back downhill to the right on the same trail.

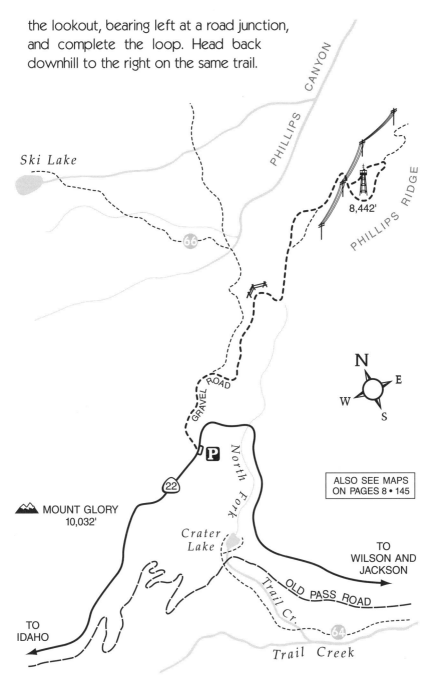

Ski Lake

PHILLIPS CANYON

PHILLIPS RIDGE

8,442'

GRAVEL ROAD

P

22

North Fork

N
W   E
S

ALSO SEE MAPS
ON PAGES 8 • 145

MOUNT GLORY
10,032'

Crater
Lake

TO
WILSON AND
JACKSON

Trail Cr.

OLD PASS ROAD

TO
IDAHO

Trail Creek

PHILLIPS RIDGE

Hike 66
Phillips Canyon and Ski Lake

Hiking distance: 4 miles round trip
Hiking time: 2 hours
Elevation gain: 900 feet
Maps: U.S.G.S. Rendezvous Peak
        Trails Illustrated Grand Teton National Park

Summary of hike: Phillips Canyon sits between Mount Glory and Phillips Ridge near Teton Pass at the south end of the Teton Range. This hike leads to Ski Lake, a circular, deep blue lake tucked into a mountain cirque on the west end of Phillips Canyon. Along the way, the trail winds through a lodgepole pine forest and an open meadow bursting with wildflowers. Phillips Canyon opens out into this meadow. The trail winds past the canyon, crossing a beautiful stream en route to Ski Lake. From the lake are views of the Gros Ventre Range in the east and the Jackson Hole valley.

Driving directions: From Jackson, head south on Highway 89 for 1.3 miles to Highway 22. Turn right and drive 1.4 miles to Wilson. Continue 4.1 miles past Wilson to the posted Phillips Canyon trailhead on the right side of the road. On the left side is a parking area. Turn left and park.

Hiking directions: Walk across the highway to the Phillips Canyon Road. Hike up the gravel road under a canopy of fir trees for 0.4 miles to a signed junction on the left. There is a Forest Service sign pointing the way to Ski Lake. The trail is a steady uphill climb but not steep. At one mile the trail drops into a beautiful flat meadow with wildflowers and a stream running through it. Continue to a signed trail fork at 1.2 miles. The Phillips Canyon Trail heads off to the right over Phillips Pass. Take the left fork beside the creek through the open forest of aspens and fir. Cross the outlet stream of Ski Lake, soon reaching the east shore of the lake. After enjoying the surroundings, take the same trail back to the trailhead.

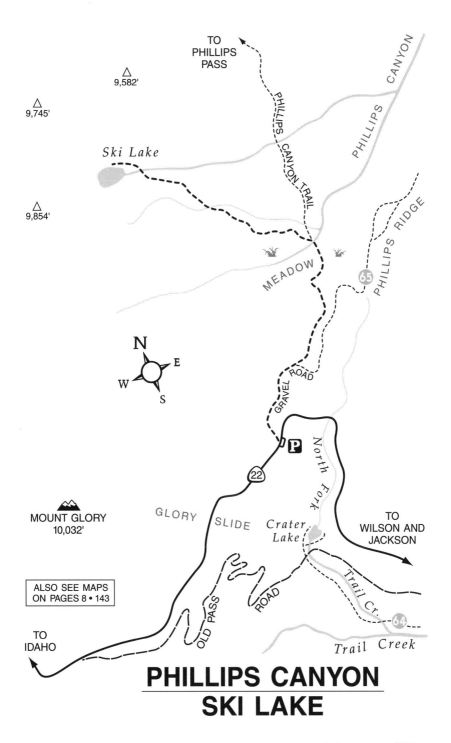

TO
PHILLIPS
PASS

△
9,582'

△
9,745'

PHILLIPS CANYON

PHILLIPS CANYON TRAIL

Ski Lake

△
9,854'

PHILLIPS RIDGE

MEADOW

65

N
E
W
S

GRAVEL ROAD

P

North Fork

22

MOUNT GLORY
10,032'

GLORY SLIDE

Crater Lake

TO
WILSON AND
JACKSON

ALSO SEE MAPS
ON PAGES 8 • 143

OLD PASS ROAD

Trail Cr.

64

TO
IDAHO

Trail Creek

PHILLIPS CANYON
SKI LAKE

Hike 67
Pass Ridge Trail

Hiking distance: 4 miles round trip
Hiking time: 2 hours
Elevation gain: 850 feet
Maps: U.S.G.S. Teton Pass
Trails Illustrated Grand Teton National Park

Summary of hike: Teton Pass is the divide separating the Teton Range to the north and the Snake River Range to the south. The Pass Ridge Trail follows a ridge along the Snake River Range. The trail begins at the pass and heads up to a 9,279-foot summit, passing through meadows covered in wildflowers and a forested hillside. Along the trail are great views of the Jackson Hole valley, the Snake River, and the Gros Ventre Range to the east. At the summit are views to the south of the Salt River Range, the Wyoming Range, and the South Rim.

Driving directions: From Jackson, head south on Highway 89 for 1.3 miles to Highway 22. Turn right and drive 1.4 miles to Wilson. Continue 5.6 miles past Wilson to the Teton Pass summit. The trailhead parking area is on the left.

Hiking directions: From the east end of the parking area, hike south up the hill past the trail sign. The trail climbs 200 feet up the ridge to a radio tower, where the trail intersects with a gravel service road. Hike 100 feet up the road to where the road curves off to the right and the footpath continues straight ahead, due south. At one mile, the trail enters an Engelmann spruce and subalpine fir forest. A series of switchbacks lead up to the meadows. As you near the ridge, several side paths head off to the left to overlooks of the valley below. The trail parallels the cliffs, reaching the ridge at the summit for stunning views at the head of Black Canyon. This is our turnaround spot. Return along the same path.

To hike further the trail continues 80 yards to the right before descending into Black Canyon. The trail makes a wide

4-mile sweep back to the Old Pass Road and the trailhead for Hike 64 (see inset map).

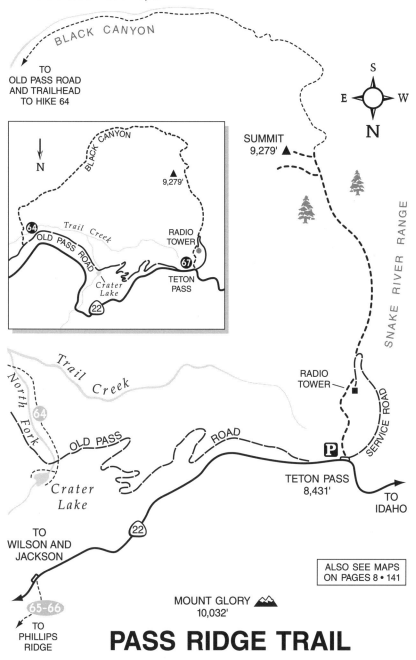

BLACK CANYON

TO
OLD PASS ROAD
AND TRAILHEAD
TO HIKE 64

S
E ⊕ W
N

SUMMIT
9,279' ▲

SNAKE RIVER RANGE

N

BLACK CANYON

▲
9,279'

Trail Creek

RADIO
TOWER

64
OLD PASS ROAD

67

Crater Lake

TETON
PASS

22

Trail Creek

North Fork

64

OLD PASS ROAD

Crater Lake

RADIO
TOWER ■

SERVICE ROAD

P

TETON PASS
8,431'

TO
IDAHO

22

TO
WILSON AND
JACKSON

ALSO SEE MAPS
ON PAGES 8 • 141

65-66

TO
PHILLIPS
RIDGE

MOUNT GLORY ⛰
10,032'

PASS RIDGE TRAIL

Hike 68
Coal Creek Trail

Hiking distance: 4.4 miles round trip
Hiking time: 2.5 hours
Elevation gain: 700 feet
Maps: U.S.G.S. Rendezvous Peak

Summary of hike: The Coal Creek Trail parallels Coal Creek along the southern slopes of the Teton Mountains from the Idaho side of Teton Pass. The drainage is nestled between Taylor Mountain and Mount Glory in the Jedediah Smith Wilderness. The lightly used trail leads through a beautiful backcountry area to Coal Creek Meadows in an open bowl. The hike has a steady elevation gain all the way to the meadow.

Driving directions: From Jackson, head south on Highway 89 for 1.3 miles to Highway 22. Turn right and drive 1.4 miles to Wilson. Continue 8.2 miles past Wilson, over Teton Pass, to the Coal Creek trailhead parking area on the right.

Hiking directions: The trail heads north past the trailhead sign at the mouth of the canyon through meadows with stands of subalpine fir. Cross a log bridge over Coal Creek. Continue up the draw, entering the Jedediah Smith Wilderness in the shadow of Taylor Mountain. The trail continues along the northwest bank of the cascading creek to another creek crossing at 1.1 mile. After crossing, the trail leaves the creek, curving to the right through an aspen grove on the east slopes. The gradient steepens as the trail curves left, again heading north. Continue uphill to a ridge at 2.2 miles where the trail levels out in Coal Creek Meadows. This tree-lined meadow is the turnaround spot. Return on the same trail.

To hike further, continue to the north end of the meadow and a junction. The left fork heads west over Taylor Mountain, climbing 1,000 feet in one mile. The right fork heads north, climbing to the 9,197-foot Mesquite Creek Divide. The trail then follows Mesquite and Moose Creeks to the Teton Crest Trail.

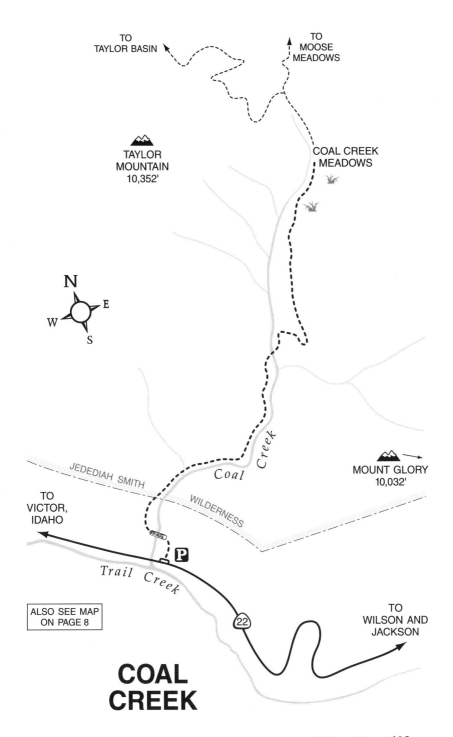

TO
TAYLOR BASIN

TO
MOOSE
MEADOWS

TAYLOR
MOUNTAIN
10,352'

COAL CREEK
MEADOWS

N
W E
S

Creek

Coal

MOUNT GLORY
10,032'

JEDEDIAH SMITH

WILDERNESS

TO
VICTOR,
IDAHO

P

Trail Creek

TO
WILSON AND
JACKSON

22

ALSO SEE MAP
ON PAGE 8

COAL
CREEK

Hike 69
Game Creek Loop

Hiking distance: 7.4 miles round trip
Hiking time: 3.5 hours
Elevation gain: 200 feet
Maps: U.S.G.S. Cache Creek

Summary of hike: Game Creek flows through a beautiful, near-level canyon in the Gros Ventre Mountains south of Jackson. Small streams snake through the lower meadow, marbled with marshes and abundant with wildflowers. This loop hike takes in the first 3.7 miles of the Game Creek Trail in the pastoral mountain valley. The trail winds through the wetland meadow while staying on dry land. The hike can be combined with the Cache Creek Trail (Hike 61) for a 11.7-mile one-way shuttle.

Driving directions: Drive 7.5 miles south of Jackson on Highway 89. Between mile markers 146 and 147, turn left on Game Creek Road. Drive one mile to a sharp right bend in the road. Within the bend is the posted trailhead parking area on the left.

Hiking directions: Walk 30 yards back down the road to the gravel road on the right. Head east on the gravel road, past the trailhead gate, just inside the Teton National Forest. Follow the old road up the open canyon between the tree-dotted hills with rock outcroppings, parallel to the north bank of Game Creek. The road crosses the creek, then curves north. Cross a cattle guard, steadily gaining elevation to the old trailhead by a buck fence at 2.2 miles. Cross the footbridge over Game Creek, and traverse the base of the hillside on the west edge of the meadow. The path remains raised above the wetland meadow, marbled with meandering streams. When the trail crosses through a tributary stream, use the bridge in the brush to the left. Forty yards after crossing, the road narrows to a footpath and curves right, crossing to the east side of Game Creek at a T-junction. The return route is to the right. For now, head up canyon to the left. Cross a small bridge over a feeder stream, continuing 0.2 miles to a junction with a bridge on the left. This is our turnaround spot. On the return, the footpath follows the east edge of the valley on a gradual downhill slope. Complete the loop 100 yards below the buck fence at the old trailhead.

To hike further from the turnaround spot, the left fork crosses the bridge over Game Creek and leads to Wilson Canyon, Leeks Canyon, and Snow King Mountain above the town of Jackson. The Game Creek Trail continues on the right fork to the Cache Creek Trail (Hike 61).

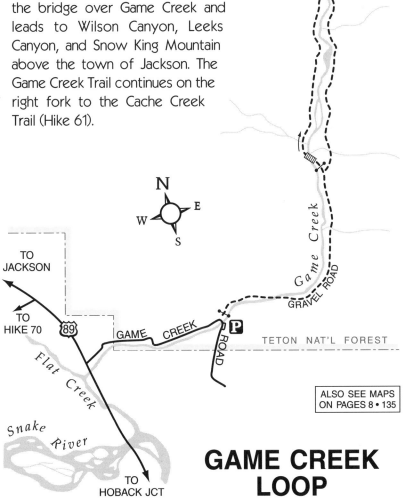

TO
CACHE CREEK
(HIKE 61)

TO
SNOW KING
MOUNTAIN

N

W   E

S

TO
JACKSON

TO
HIKE 70

89

GAME   CREEK

Game Creek

GRAVEL ROAD

ROAD

P

TETON NAT'L FOREST

Flat Creek

Snake River

TO
HOBACK JCT

ALSO SEE MAPS
ON PAGES 8 • 135

GAME CREEK
LOOP

Hike 70
South Park
BIG GAME WINTER RANGE

Hiking distance: 2.5 miles round trip
Hiking time: 1.5 hours
Elevation gain: Level
Maps: U.S.G.S. Jackson

Summary of hike: South Park runs north and south in the flatlands south of Jackson. Flat Creek, Spring Creek, and the numerous channels of the Snake River slowly wind through the verdant valley, bordered on the west by the Snake River Range and on the east by the Gros Ventre Range. This hike loops through the riparian wetland valley with mountain views in every direction. The trail crosses streams and strolls along the Snake River through a large stand of cottonwood trees. There are picnic areas along the river.

The area is managed by the Wyoming Game and Fish Department. It provides the elk a winter range and feeding ground. During spring and summer it is a bird habitat for feeding, nesting, and raising young.

Driving directions: From downtown Jackson, drive 7 miles south on Highway 89. Turn right by the "South Park" sign. Drive one mile down into the valley, and park at the end of the road by the hay sheds and the bridge.

Hiking directions: Pass the trailhead gate and cross the bridge over Flat Creek. Take the level trail to the left across the meadow and past the log corral towards the cottonwood trees at the Snake River. On the left is the old Davis homestead log cabin, built in 1902. Head right on the trail, following the watercourse alongside the Snake River and through the forest. After exploring the shoreline, take the jeep trail that loops back through the meadow. Recross the bridge at the barns and parking area.

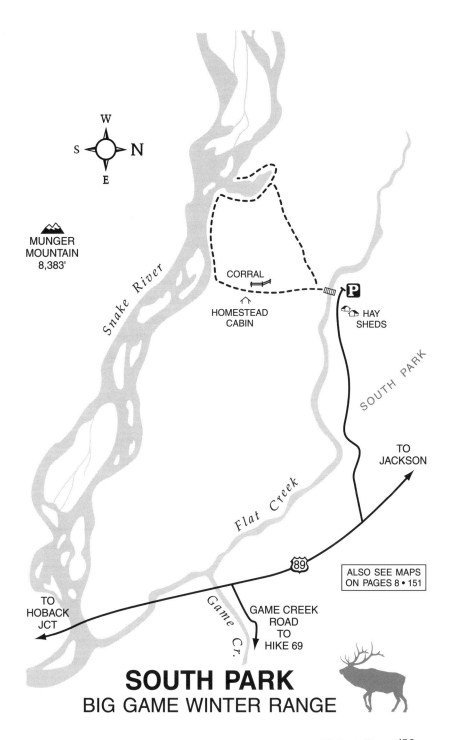

W
S ✦ N
E

MUNGER
MOUNTAIN
8,383'

Snake River

CORRAL

HOMESTEAD
CABIN

P

HAY
SHEDS

SOUTH PARK

Flat Creek

TO
JACKSON

89

ALSO SEE MAPS
ON PAGES 8 • 151

TO
HOBACK
JCT

Game Cr.

GAME CREEK
ROAD
TO
HIKE 69

SOUTH PARK
BIG GAME WINTER RANGE

Hike 71
Dog Creek Trail

Hiking distance: 4.4 miles round trip
Hiking time: 2.5 hours
Elevation gain: 300 feet
Maps: U.S.G.S. Munger Mountain

Summary of hike: Dog Creek, in the remote Snake River Range, flows down a lush canyon and joins the Snake River south of Hoback Junction. The Dog Creek Trail heads up the canyon parallel to the creek through an endless garden of wildflowers. Moose and elk are frequently seen in this drainage.

Driving directions: From Jackson, drive south on Highway 89 for 14 miles to Hoback Junction and take the right fork, staying on Highway 89. Drive 4.8 miles to an unsigned turnoff on the right, located 0.5 miles past the posted Wilson-Fall Creek Road turnoff. Make a sharp right turn. Follow the narrow dirt road 0.4 miles, crossing a bridge over Pritchard Creek on the south edge of Pritchard Pond, to the posted trailhead and parking area by the old corral.

Hiking directions: From the posted trailhead at the mouth of the canyon, take the forested path uphill. Follow the open slopes on the north side of Dog Creek, with views of Wolf Mountain straight ahead. Cross a couple of feeder streams to a junction at one mile. The left fork leads to Cabin Creek and Wolf Mountain. Stay to the right and continue northwest to a junction at 2.2 miles, by the confluence of Dog Creek and Little Dog Creek. This is our turnaround spot.

To hike further, the left fork continues up Dog Creek to Red Pass and Wolf Mountain. The right fork follows Little Dog Creek a short distance and heads north along Pup Creek.

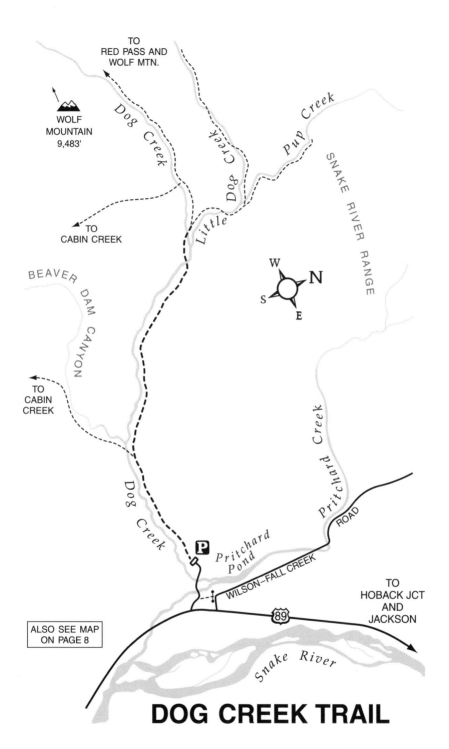

TO
RED PASS AND
WOLF MTN.

WOLF
MOUNTAIN
9,483'

Dog Creek

Little Dog Creek

Pup Creek

SNAKE RIVER RANGE

TO
CABIN CREEK

BEAVER DAM CANYON

TO
CABIN
CREEK

W N
S E

Dog Creek

Pritchard Creek

Pritchard Pond

ROAD

P

WILSON–FALL CREEK

89

TO
HOBACK JCT
AND
JACKSON

ALSO SEE MAP
ON PAGE 8

Snake River

DOG CREEK TRAIL

Hike 72
Granite Falls and Hot Springs

Hiking distance: 1 mile round trip
Hiking time: 30 minutes plus soaking time
Elevation gain: 300 feet
Maps: U.S.G.S. Granite Falls

Summary of hike: Granite Falls and Hot Springs are located in the Gros Ventre Mountains east of Hoback Junction. This short hike follows Granite Creek as it cascades over magnificent Granite Falls, a wide, roaring 20-foot cascade. The waterfall was used as a backdrop in the movie *A River Runs Through It.* The trail begins at an elevation of 7,000 feet by Granite Hot Springs, a developed hot springs built in 1933 with changing rooms and a 45 x 75-foot pool. The hike follows the cascading creek downstream to Granite Falls Hot Springs, a primitive hot springs on the edge of the creek at the base of Granite Falls.

Driving directions: From Jackson, drive south 14 miles on Highway 89 to the Hoback Junction. Take the left fork (Highway 191/189) towards Pinedale. Drive 11.5 miles to the Granite Recreational Area turnoff. A large sign marks the turn. Turn left and drive 10 miles on a gravel road to Granite Hot Springs. Park in the lot at the end of the road.

Hiking directions: Walk through the gate and across the river towards Granite Hot Springs. To get to Granite Falls, take the right trail along the east side of the creek. As you hike, you will see the powerful Granite Creek swiftly tumbling towards the falls and a view down the Granite Creek valley. Past the falls, take the steep trail to the right, descending down to the creek. At the creek is the hot springs and a primitive soaking pool 50 yards in front of the falls. To return, retrace your steps back to Granite Hot Springs.

Taking the left (north) trail at the beginning of the hike leads through a beautiful forest into the canyon. Moose frequent the meadow that is just 15 minutes from the trailhead. This trail is part of a much longer trail leading northwest to Turquoise Lake (11 miles) and Cache Creek in Jackson (17 miles).

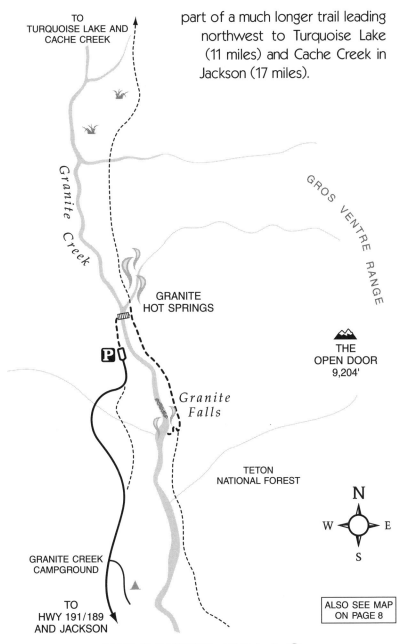

TO
TURQUOISE LAKE AND
CACHE CREEK

Granite Creek

GROS VENTRE RANGE

GRANITE
HOT SPRINGS

THE
OPEN DOOR
9,204'

P

Granite
Falls

TETON
NATIONAL FOREST

N
W ← → E
S

GRANITE CREEK
CAMPGROUND

TO
HWY 191/189
AND JACKSON

ALSO SEE MAP
ON PAGE 8

GRANITE FALLS
GRANITE HOT SPRINGS

DAY HIKE BOOKS

These books may be purchased at your local bookstore or
outdoor shop. Or, order them direct from the distributor:

The Globe Pequot Press

246 Goose Lane • P.O. Box 480 • Guilford, CT 06437-0480
on the web: www.globe-pequot.com

800-243-0495 DIRECT   **800-820-2329** FAX